Author: Yu Aikawa
Translator: Jason Tanthum
English Adaptation: Gayle Tan
Supervising Editor: Matthew Scrivner
Production: DGN Production, Inc.
V.P of Operations: Yuki Chung
President: Jennifer Chen

Publisher
DrMaster Publications, Inc.
4044 Clipper Ct.
Fremont, CA 94538
www.drmasterbooks.com

First Edition: July 2008

ISBN 13: 978-1-59796-028-1

INDEX

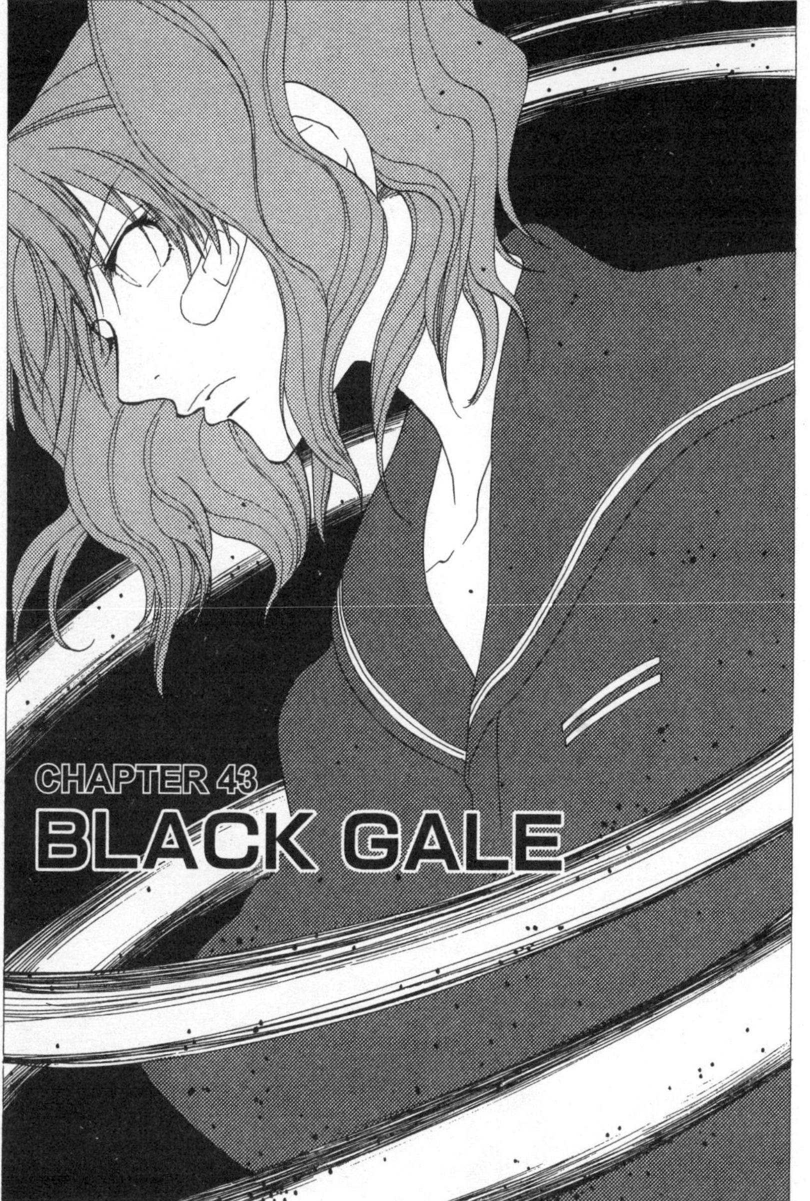
CHAPTER 43
BLACK GALE

NO...
THAT SORT OF CREATURE DOESN'T EXIST IN THIS WORLD ...

NOW ...
PLEASE ...
FORGET ...

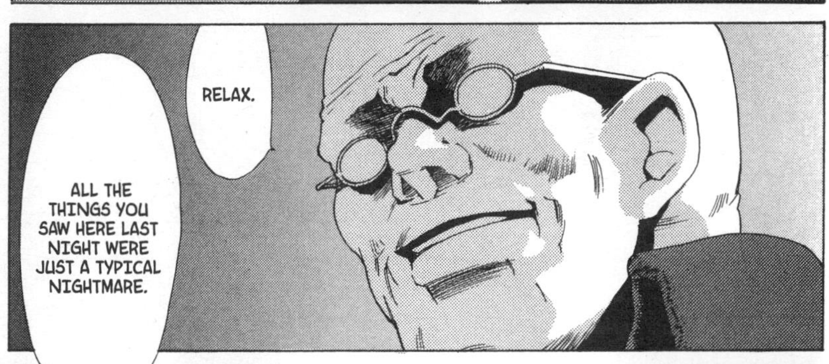

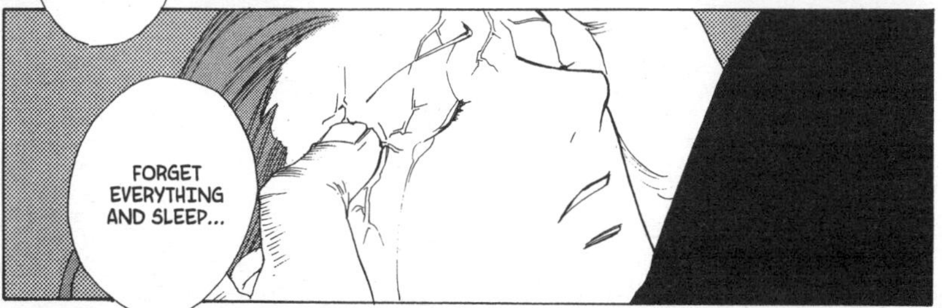

PRINCIPAL.
HAS KIKUCHI SAN REALLY ...?

YES.
BOTH WHAT HAPPENED TONIGHT AND LAST NIGHT...
SHE'LL REMEMBER NONE OF IT.
...

I'LL OPEN THE SCHOOL GATES NOW.
PLEASE TAKE KIKUCHI-SAN AND LEAVE QUICKLY.
ALREADY?

BEFORE SHE WAKES UP...
...AND ONCE AGAIN SEES THE SHAPE THIS SCHOOL TAKES AT NIGHT.

WELL,
I FULFILLED YOUR REQUEST.
NOW IT'S YOUR TURN TO LISTEN TO MY REQUEST,
MAO-SAMA.

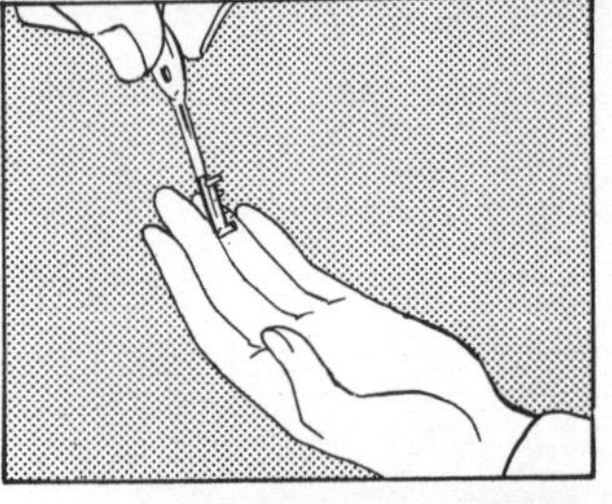

YOU GUYS, ARE YOU REALLY GOING HOME?
WE DON'T HAVE A CHOICE.
That baldy has a lot of power, doesn't he?
YOU SAY GO HOME, BUT WE HAVE TO TAKE KIKUCHI-SAN OUTSIDE FIRST.
I'll carry her.
Far away.
It's okay. I can do it myself.

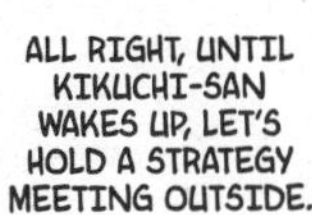

MORE STUDENTS DID DIE YESTERDAY, AFTER ALL...
CAPTURE THEM ONE BY ONE? AIN'T THAT INTERESTING?
I'm in.
ARE YOU GOING TO PLAY TONIGHT TOO, YOSHIKUNI?

HMM?
It's been a while, huh?
It hasn't been long at all.
IS THAT HOW IT IS?
WHOOSH
WE CAN LEAVE KIKUCHI-SAN TO SOMEONE ELSE.
STOP IT, YOSHIKUNI.
CAN'T IT WAIT UNTIL TOMORROW?

WHAT ARE YOU THINKING, ISE...?
WHAT YOU DO IS FINE, BUT DON'T INVOLVE OTHERS.
NISHIWAKI STILL DOESN'T UNDERSTAND?
Damn, the security here sucks.
EVEN WITH THE MARK OF A NOSFERATU COVERING THE ENTIRE SHAPE OF HIS BODY...

WELL, YOU COULD SAY FOR YOU CARRIERS AND FOR SHIMIZU AND I, WHO HAVE BEEN CHARMED BY THE NOSFERATU,

THERE ARE OTHER PLACES TO BE AT NIGHT BESIDES THIS SCHOOL...

WHERE ON CAMPUS AM I...?
IT'S TOO DARK TO SEE ANYTHING ...

FLAP
FLAP
...!

HOW PERSISTENT!

SWISH

SHOW YOURSELF!

SWISH

SWISH

CRUNCH

WHOOSH

SPURT

OW!

JERK

DRAG ズルズル
WAIT... WHO ARE YOU?!
WHAT ARE YOU DOING? LET GO!
I SHOULD HAVE TOLD YOU TO GO INSIDE.
WHY WERE YOU CIRCLING THE SOUTH SIDE?
TSUCHIYA!
SQUEEZE
CREAK
CREAK
...

...UMM, HEY...
I WAS FEELING HORRIBLE BECAUSE YOU DIDN'T SHOW.
DIFFERENT FROM FEELING PLEASURE?

...YOU SAVED US FROM NOGI AND THE OTHERS... AND EVEN NOW...

THERE ARE TWO REASONS MY CONDUCT DIFFERS LARGELY FROM OTHER NOSFERATU.
I TAKE ACTIONS IN ORDER TO PROTECT MY EVIL GENES
AND TO FIND GOOD SUBJECTS INTO WHICH TO SPREAD MY EVIL GENES.

I LONG FOR THE NIGHT WHEN TAKAGI FINALLY DIES, AND I'M ABLE TO FEED ONCE AGAIN.

AT THE SAME TIME, I NEED TO SECURE PEOPLE OFF OF WHOM I CAN FEED.

SCRATCH

SO... IN OTHER WORDS... EVEN NOW...

I...?

SHATTER

YOU DARE ENTER MY TERRITORY?!

BLAM

WHY? THEY'RE LIKE ZOMBIES, BUT...

BLAM

BLAM

They keep circling the windows on the north side as if brainless.

This is where Kurou-chan was being confined by Satou before...

DID THEY SUDDENLY GET THEIR HANDS ON SOME STRONGER-THAN-NORMAL EVIL GENES?

THE SCENT OF THE EVIL GENES IS NO DIFFERENT FROM BEFORE. THEY HAVE THE SCENT OF ZOMBIES CREATED BY SATOU.

THUD

BLAM

HOWEVER, THERE'S SOMETHING ELSE... NOT EVIL GENES, BUT THE SCENT OF SOMETHING ORDINARY IS MIXED IN.

ORDINARY? WHAT DO YOU MEAN BY ORDINARY?
YEAH.
I GET THE FEELING I'VE SMELLED IT BEFORE.
THE PERSON WHO TORE APART ALL THE ZOMBIES IS PROBABLY THE ONE WHO'S CURRENTLY TAKING THIS FORM.
MOREOVER, THEY AREN'T NOSFERATU. NOSFERATU DON'T ATTACK THEIR OWN FAMILY.

IS THAT SO? THEN WHAT ARE THEY?
ALSO, DO NOSFERATU NOT ATTACK CARRIERS?

THUD
ALSO, I HAVE NO INTEREST IN PEOPLE INJECTED WITH EVIL GENES.
BLAM
THE ONLY THINGS NOSFERATU ARE INTERESTED IN ARE TASTY HUMANS.

I'VE NEVER KILLED ONE BEFORE.
THEY TASTE AWFUL...
BLAM

AND I'M A BIT INTERESTED IN YOU AT THE MOMENT.
Your type clearly does not possess an outspoken determination.
HUH?!
1
AREN'T YOU SOMEWHAT MISTAKEN?

I'M DIFFERENT FROM OKAMOTO!
I'M NOT ALL "I WANT TO DIE!" OR "I DON'T CARE WHAT HAPPENS TO ME!"
I'M NOT THAT KIND OF PERSON!

THAT'S RIGHT, HUH?
There is no opposite sex among Nosferatu!
HONESTLY, PEOPLE WITHOUT LIFE-FORCE DON'T FALL IN LOVE WITH THE OPPOSITE SEX.
!
RELAX. TAKAGI IS A PROPER HUMAN MALE.
It's true love.
It's out...
WELL THEN, WHY?!
WHAT'S THE REASON I'VE CAUGHT YOUR EYE?!
...YOU SAY YOU'RE DIFFERENT FROM OKAMOTO, BUT...
THE LINE BETWEEN THOSE WHO WANT TO BE DESTROYED AND THOSE WHO WANT TO DO THE DESTROYING IS PAPER-THIN

DESTROY YOUR HOUSE? WHY?

IN ANY CASE, I THOUGHT I'D MESS THINGS UP.

THAT'S WHY...

UMM...
SENSEI, I...
I DON'T KNOW WHY, BUT WHEN I WAS IN MIDDLE-SCHOOL,
AND I SAW THE BACK OF A BOY WALKING IN FRONT OF ME,
MY HEART STARTED BEATING FOR NO REASON, AND I WANTED TO BEAT HIM UP.
AND THEN...
I DIDN'T CARE ABOUT MY PARENTS, LET ALONE HATE THEM,
BUT I THOUGHT ABOUT DESTROYING MY HOUSE, AND I DON'T KNOW WHY.
AND SO, WITH ALL OUR MIGHT, OKAMOTO AND I
WRECKED EACH OTHER'S HOUSES.

WHILE EVERYONE IN OKAMOTO'S HOUSE WAS GONE, I MESSED EVERYTHING UP.

AFTER THAT, WE BOTH CAME OUT.

THE POLICE DIDN'T GET INVOLVED, BUT... WELL, THERE WAS THE CHILD CONSULTATION CENTER AND COUNSELING AND OTHER THINGS...

SO WE BOTH REPEATED A GRADE.

WHEN WE BOTH BECAME HIGH-SCHOOL STUDENTS, WE PROMISED TO HAVE AS MUCH FUN AS ALWAYS.

BUT...

YOU KILLED OKAMOTO!
THAT'S RIGHT.
Straight forward.
...
WELL, EVEN THOUGH YOU'RE NOT HUMAN, I FIND IT EASY TO TALK TO YOU.
IT'S STRA-NGE ...
What am I saying to this guy?

BUT... SOMEHOW ...
YOU DID HORRIBLE THINGS TO OKAMOTO... WHO LOVED ONLY ME...
IN THE END, ISN'T IT ALL YOUR FAULT?!
Honest and straightforward.
THAT'S RIGHT.
IF TAKAGI HAD DIED AT THAT OPPORTUNE TIME...
I WOULD HAVE TAKEN YOU TO THE SAME PLACE AS OKAMOTO...
Ikezukuri or shiokara*? Take your pick!
TAKEN WHO?!
KUROU-CHAN
DEFIN-ITELY
WON'T LET ME
SUFFER THROUGH SOMETHING LIKE DEATH!

*Ikezukuri is slices of fresh raw fish arranged to look lifelike. Shiokara is fish guts pickled in sea salt. Either way, she's threatening to disembowel him.

Spends his days absorbing Japanese culture.↑

HURRY!
THEY'LL CLOSE SOON!
WHEW! I'M ALL TINGLY!
It can't be helped. We're carriers.
For sure.
It's only natural.
Once we leave the gates ...

GEEZ, NOW WHAT? WE MISSED THE LAST TRAIN, SO ARE WE CAMPING HERE UNTIL MORNING?
I CAN'T VERY WELL WALK HOME LIKE THIS.
If my dad wakes up, then...
YOU'RE GONNA HAVE TO HIDE THAT FACE AGAIN?
JUST MAKING SURE.

WELL, I'LL GO FOR A BIT AND TRY CALLING.
STOP!
IT'S NOT GOOD TO CONCERN YOURSELF WITH ISE.
HE HAS A LITTLE BIT OF A... DANGEROUS MINDSET.
DO YOU HAVE A PROBLEM WITH ISE?
If so, don't rush in.
YOU SAY HE'S DANGEROUS, BUT HE'S PROBABLY ONLY SELFISH.
...WELL, IN ANY CASE, LEAVE IT BE, TAKAGI.
RUMBLE
AHH! THE GATE'S CLOSING!

RUMBLE
RUMBLE
TAKAGI!
WAIT, TAKAGI-KUN!
I'LL BE ALL RIGHT!
ANYWAY, YOU THREE START THINKING!
ABOUT TOMORROW'S TAKEOVER...
RUMBLE
HE WENT...
WELL... TAKAGI'S THAT KIND OF PERSON...

HEY, TAKAGI! TAKE AT LEAST ONE BODYGUARD WITH YOU!
WHAT, YOU LEFT THE THREE CARRIERS BEHIND OUT HERE?
HAA...
IT'S OKAY! HE HAS POCHI WITH HIM!
PHEW!
DIDN'T IT SEEM LIKE SONOBE-SENSEI WAS ALREADY STUFFED TONIGHT?
AND SATOU-SENSEI LIKES US AND WON'T ATTACK.

SHUT
CREAK
CREAK
THE WIND...
DID IT OPEN THE WINDOWS...?

RAT-
TLE
FWOOSH
WITHOUT THE ZOMBIES HERE... IT'S QUIET TONIGHT...

...I LOVE THE DARK...
...I FEEL RELAXED ...

...SPEAKING OF WHICH, I HAVE TO TALK TO SATOU REGARDING THE AFTERMATH OF THE COFFIN INCIDENT ...

SENSEI'S PROBABLY HERE?

IF IT WON'T OPEN, I'LL BREAK DOWN THE DOOR.

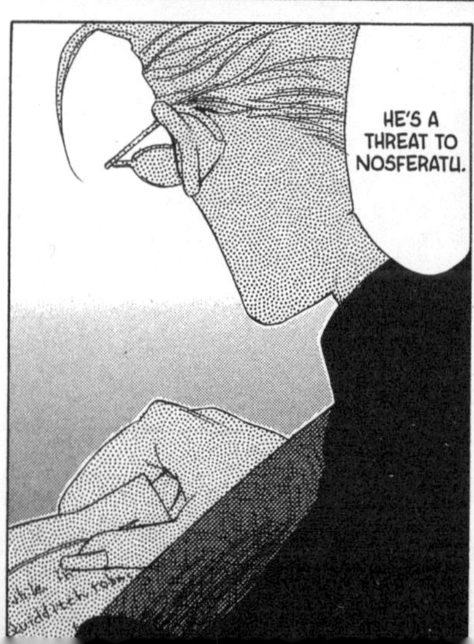

EVEN IF YOU BREAK DOWN THE DOOR, YOU CAN'T ENTER.

HAS THAT GUY DRAWN OUT A TYPICAL BARRIER?

THAT'S A VERY TSUCHIYA TACTIC...

BUT...

IF HIS STOMACH IS EMPTY, HE'LL COME...

CLICK

CLICK

CLICK

GRAB
...
UGH...
HA...
...
AREN'T YOU HUNGRY?!
COME OUT!

CREAK

The main characters File 1:

MIKI AKASAKA

A hot-blooded female student. Okamoto, who was turned into a zombie, was her best friend since elementary school. At the age of sixteen, she is a year older than Kurou and the others. She's beginning to fall in love with Kurou, but because of the influence of the "coffin," she hates herself for forgetting about him. She sustained serious injuries in the fight against the zombie students, but she received treatment from Fukaya and survived. While hospitalized, Touyama left her with a key and a Japanese sword that can only cut Nosferatu.

KUROU TAKAGI

The main character. After losing his mother, he became a transfer student at Yotsuji Acadamy, run by his father of whom he has no memory. While there, he entered the "coffin" and his existence was completely forgotten, but the sacrifice of his twin sister, Suemi, allowed him to escape. As a result, the previously united male and female "Nosferatu seeds" were divided. With just the male seed remaining, the only requirement for him to become the King of the Nosferatu is his death. He has Pochi as a familiar.

RUI NISHWAKI

Born from a Japanese father and an American mother. Excels at studies. Though he has a large frame, he is also clever enough to draw maps of the school. He was drawn into the Coffin of Oblivion by the history teacher, Matsudaira, but was able to escape when Kurou became his substitute. Afterwards, he was tricked by Matsudaira into inheriting his evil genes and became a Carrier. Also, at night, the mark of the Nosferatu appears all over his body.

KOUICHI YOSHIKUNI

A dangerous man who subconsciously likes perilous situations, he often loses himself and goes on rampages. Because of a rumor that he killed someone when he was in middle school, he was recently dumped by his girlfriend, who was a year older. With the zombie Okamoto's evil genes transferred into him, he now commands fire, becoming a Carrier whose only existence is to kill and wound Nosferatu. After that, the school became a playground for him. He's in love with Mao Touyama.

CHAPTER 44
HEAVEN'S BREATH

SHUT

YOU HAD THE RESOLUTION TO COME HERE.
THOUGH THAT WOUND LOOKS DESPERATELY SHALLOW...

NATURALLY, I COULDN'T CUT ANY DEEPER THAN THIS.
I WOULD DIE OTHERWISE.
It hurts enough.

HONESTLY SPEAKING, I MYSELF DON'T HAVE THE STRENGTH TO INCREASE THE NUMBER OF NOSFERATU.
DO YOU UNDERSTAND WHY?

IF I ONLY LET HIM SMELL THE BLOOD...
...IT SHOULD EASILY BE ENOUGH TO LET ME INSIDE.

PROBABLY
BECAUSE YOU HATE NOSFERATU, SENSEI.

IF I BECOME A NOSFERATU, WILL I REGRET IT?
WILL I HATE KILLING HUMANS?

IS ASKING THESE MANY QUESTIONS WHILE CONTINUING TO LIVE FOR ETERNITY PAINFUL?

I WON'T HAVE ANY REGRETS!
I'LL LIKE EATING PEOPLE AS LONG AS THEY'RE DELICIOUS!

I WILL NOT EAT STUDENTS.

WHETHER THEY BECOME NOSFERATU, ZOMBIES, OR CARRIERS,
I HAVE A MORE IMPORTANT ROLE TO THE STUDENTS OF THIS SCHOOL...

ROLE...? WHAT DO YOU MEAN, ROLE?
...THAT HAS NOTHING TO DO WITH YOU.

SOMEONE'S TRYING TO TREAD IN ON MY TERRITORY.
SLAM
!

CERTAINLY... I'VE DEFINITELY NOTICED...
THE SMELL OF ISE-KUN'S BLOOD IS ...

WHERE DO I REMEMBER SMELLING IT BEFORE?
I'VE SURELY ENCOUNTERED IT BEFORE...

IS IT OKAY TO DRINK IT? I'M SO TEMPTED.
WHAT, HAVEN'T YOU BEEN FULLY INTERESTED IN ME FROM THE START?
Haha.
If you have the right to choose, surely you'd drink only from virgins...?

HOWEVER, AT ANY RATE, YOU SEEMED LIKE YOU'D TASTE THE WORST IN THE ENTIRE SCHOOL, ISE-KUN.
WHAT DO YOU MEAN ENTIRE SCHOOL?!
How rude!
BY THE WAY...
BUT THE TIME YOU WERE ATTACKED BY NOGI-SAN, I SECRETLY TASTED IT AND IT WAS SO TASTY THAT I WAS TREMBLING.
QUIVER
What's up with this blood?
Take that monsters!
DON'T START TASTING PEOPLE FREELY!

DOES THE TASTE EVEN MATTER?
IT ONLY TAKES ONE BITE TO TURN ME INTO A NOSFERATU!
HEY! ALL THAT SLOPPY FANFARE IS SO TROUBLESOME!

ONE BITE?
FOR ME... TO TURN YOU INTO A NOSFERATU?

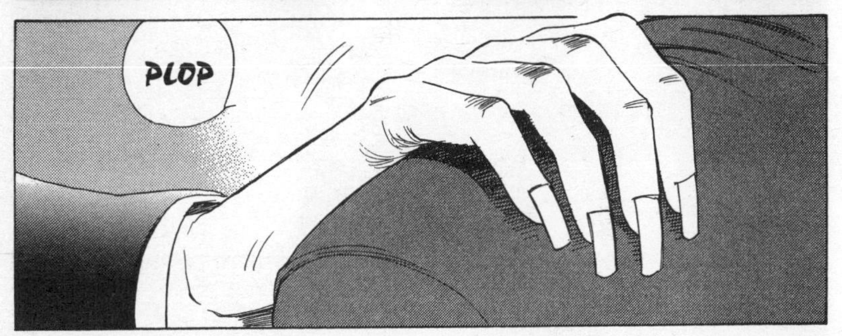
PLOP

DID YOU NOT CONSIDER ONE MORE POSSIBILITY?
I WONDER WHERE ISE WENT...
IT'S REALLY NO FUN TO BE LEFT ALL ALONE LIKE THIS...

THIS IS...

DARK...

THUD
THUD
THUD
THUD
THUD

I'm exhausted...
DAMN... I SHOULDN'T HAVE COME ALONE...
I FORGOT THERE'S A LOT OF DARK BETWEEN HERE AND THE...

SCHOOL GATES...?
FLAP
FLAP

FLAP
A BAT ...?
IN THE SCHOOL ...?
UWAAAAAAAAH!
WHAT ARE THEY ...?!
MONSTERS ...?!

!
NA...
NAKA-
YAMA-
SENSEI
...?!
...

FLAP
FLAP
FLAP
FLAP
PO...
POCHI... WHERE ARE YOU ...?
HELP ME...

....!

...

SEED...
WHOOSH

SEED...?

DID THEY NOT ATTACK ME BECAUSE I HAVE THE NOSFERATU SEED...?
AND EVEN SO, WHY IS NAKAYAMA-SENSEI IN THAT STATE...?

MORE IMPORTANTLY, POCHI...!
My zombie repellant!
HE DIDN'T COME OUT AT SUCH A CRUCIAL TIME...

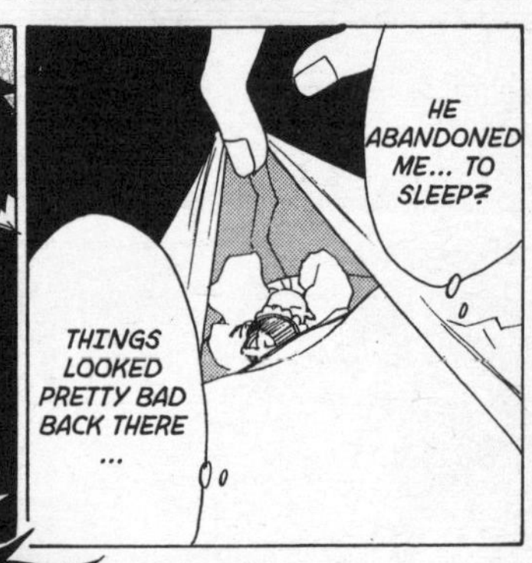
HE ABANDONED ME... TO SLEEP?
THINGS LOOKED PRETTY BAD BACK THERE ...

Ah!
IS IT THAT HE'S LULLED BY MY SCENT?!

THE SCHOOL'S SAFE...?
YOU GOTTA BE KIDDING...
IF I DON'T FIND ISE SOON...

VRRRR

HO...

HOLD ON...!

DIDN'T YOU HEAR SOMEONE'S VOICE FROM BELOW...?

DON'T TELL ME YOU'RE SCARED.

I WON'T LET YOU STALL ANY LONGER.

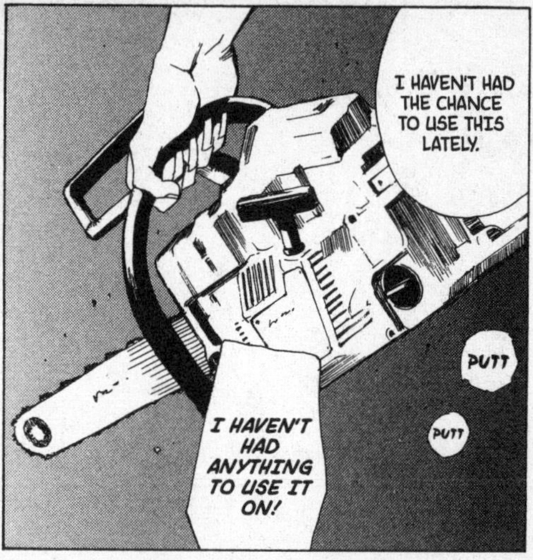
I HAVEN'T HAD THE CHANCE TO USE THIS LATELY.
I HAVEN'T HAD ANYTHING TO USE IT ON!
PUTT
PUTT

VRRRR
WA...
SERIOUSLY, STOP...

EEE...
RRRRR

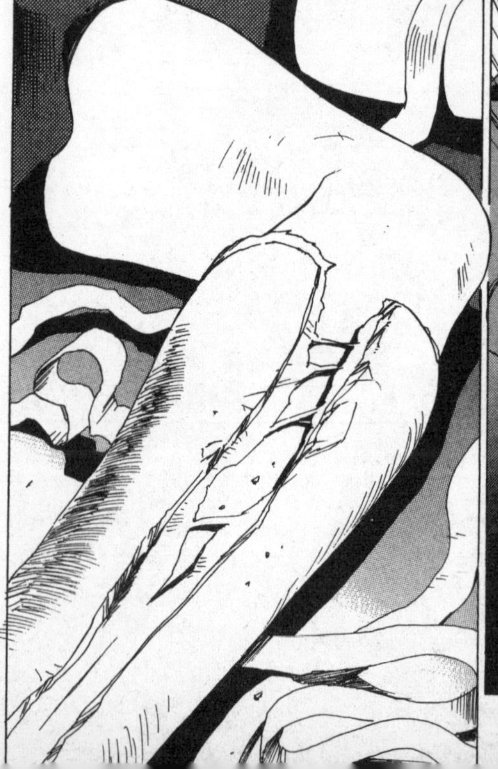

IT DOESN'T HURT, RIGHT?
Taking a cast off with a chainsaw...
SNAP
It came off as one piece.
AH, FREEDOM!
WIGGLE コキ
コキ WIGGLE
STRETCH
NOW IT WON'T BE ANNOYING TO TAKE A BATH!

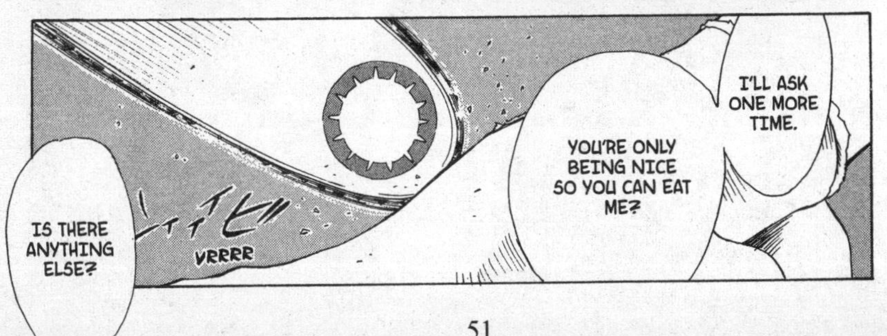

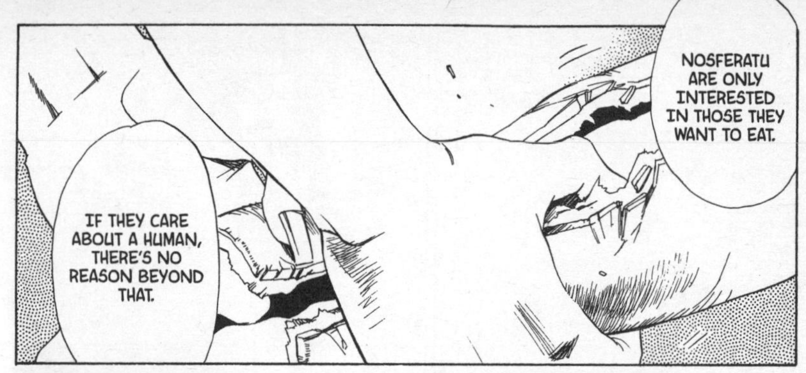
NOSFERATU ARE ONLY INTERESTED IN THOSE THEY WANT TO EAT.
IF THEY CARE ABOUT A HUMAN, THERE'S NO REASON BEYOND THAT.

YOU SAY THERE'S NO REASON, AND YOU CAN BE HONEST...
Tsuchiya...
DO OTHER NOSFERATU ALSO THINK LIKE THAT?

WELL, THE WAYS OF CARING ARE SEVERAL,
BUT THE REASONING'S THE SAME.

BUT...
SATOU...

I GET THE FEELING THAT HE'S NOTHING BUT NICE.
LUS
I HAVEN'T HEARD OF HIM EVER EATING A STUDENT...

THAT BLOOD-SUCKER IS TOO FUSSY ABOUT HIS TASTES.

HUH?

TOSS

THERE ARE COUNTLESS VARIETIES OF BLOOD...

AMONG NOSFERATU, VAMPIRES ARE PREDOMINANT AND HOLD A LOT OF POWER.
A long time ago, Tsuchiya once escaped from being bitten by a (sexy) female vampire like this.
IF VAMPIRES WERE TO FEED INDISCRIMINATELY, WE WOULD BE RUINED BY OUR MISTAKES IN THE BLINK OF AN EYE.
SO BEING FUSSY ABOUT THEIR TASTES MIGHT JUST BE INSTINCT.

THE STRONGER A NOSFERATU, THE MORE PRONOUNCED THEIR LIKES AND DISLIKES ARE.
Disgusting leech.
SO TSUCHIYA FEEDS INDISCRIMINATELY ...

SATOU IS THE TYPE TO SPECIFICALLY... RAISE HIS GAME CAREFULLY BEFORE EATING THEM.
RAISE?

THE PRECISE TEACHER DOES EXACTLY LIKE YOU'D THINK.
HE'S ALREADY LAID OUT HIS MEAL.

HE ONLY EATS OPPONENTS IN ORDER TO GAIN YOUR COMPLETE FAITH IN HIM.
BUT THEN HE SPENDS HIS TIME TAILORING THE OVERLY OUTSPOKEN STUDENTS TO BE HIS MEALS.

SO WHEN HE SAYS "I DON'T EAT STUDENTS," THAT'S JUST HIS HONED INSTINCTS.

YES...

YOU SAY SATOU IS KIND, BUT HE TAKES THE ROLE TOO SERIOUSLY.

DON'T YOU UNDERSTAND? OUR INSTINCTS ARE EQUIVALENT TO OUR NATURE.

OUR PERSONALITIES MOLD SO THAT WE MAY BETTER CATCH OUR PREY.

The people we like are influenced by our various "likes" from when we were human.

SCRATCH SCRATCH
UMM...
ISN'T LIVING LIKE THAT FUTILE?

NOSFERATU KNOW NOT OF FUTILITY.
WE PROBABLY FELT SUCH THINGS WHEN WE WERE STILL HUMAN.

AT THAT TIME ... TO BETTER SURVIVE...
IT WAS EASIER TO LIVE IN A GROUP...
UNFORTUNATELY, MY PERSONALITY DID NOT ALLOW ME TO MOLD LIKE THAT.

LIVING LIKE I DID THEN WAS PROBABLY VERY FUTILE.
I'VE ALREADY FORGOTTEN WHAT THAT FEELS LIKE.
THAT MAY BE...
THAT MAY BE... THAT MAY BE...
BUT...

I CAN'T STOMACH THE IDEA OF EVIL GENES ...

CREAK

WELL, IT'LL PROBABLY BE A WHILE BEFORE SATOU MAKES HIS MOVE ON THE STUDENTS.

IF BY SOME CHANCE HE HAS A TASTE FOR STUDENT BLOOD, HE'LL PROBABLY STILL SAY THE USUAL.

BUT SINCE VAMPIRES HAVE FUSSY TASTES,

ONCE THEY DECIDE ON A PREY, THEY WILL SURELY MOVE IN FOR THE KILL.

FLAP

FLAP

FLAP

SHIT!

IS HE GOING TO KILL ME?!

STOP PLAYING WITH ME!

I'LL NEVER BECOME A ZOMBIE!

It feels like playing Tag.

ONCE YOU SPREAD THE SCENT OF YOUR BLOOD, YOU PRESENT YOURSELF AS A MEAL.

I NEVER SAID TO EAT ME!

DIDN'T I SAY THAT ONE BITE WOULD BE ENOUGH?!

THUD
I'M AN IDIOT...
WHY... WHY DID I BELIEVE SATOU WOULDN'T KILL A HUMAN...?!
I'VE BEEN DECEIVED...!

DAMN
EVEN THOUGH I'VE SEEN HIM AT SCHOOL SEVERAL TIMES AT NIGHT,
HE'S NEVER SHOWN ANY INDICATION THAT HE'D ATTACK A STUDENT!

THERE'S NOWHERE TO RUN.
YOU'RE IN MY TERRITORY.
Someone scribbled on this rare, 16th century book...

IF I'M BITTEN, WILL I BE ABLE TO ESCAPE FAST ENOUGH...?

HONESTLY ... WHO HAS TO CLEAN THIS UP IN THE END ...?
RUMMAGE
MUTTER MUTTER
IT'S USELESS. IF HE CATCHES ME, THERE'S NO ESCAPE.
HE'S PUTTING THE BOOKS ON THE SHELVES WITH ONE ARM...!

IS IT REALLY ...
OVER FOR ME?

I...
I WANT TO GO THERE... SENSEI...

THERE?

THAT IS TO SAY...
WHERE YOU CAN REALLY...
LOOK DOWN ON HUMANS...

DID I REALLY WANT TO BECOME A NOSFERATU TO SAVE MY SISTER?

IT'S THE SAME.
IF I LOSE TSUGIKO, I CAN'T DO A THING.
IF THAT HAPPENS, I'LL BE WORTHLESS ...

SLEEP FOR A LITTLE BIT ...
THUMP
OH...
ISN'T IT GETTING HARDER TO STAY AWAKE?
ISE!
SHOCK
!
THE LIBRARY...
IS HE HERE...?

HE EASILY TRESPASSED INTO MY TERRITORY ...?!
UHMM... I'VE ALREADY CIRCLED THE ENTIRE SECOND FLOOR...
Why the library? Ise hates studying.
NEXT IS THE THIRD FLOOR...
RATTLE
BLOOD ...
IT CAN'T BE.
I'LL TRY SEARCHING DEEPER IN THE LIBRARY.

ISE?!
IF YOU'RE THERE, SAY SOMETHING!

PLEASE REMAIN DOCILE UNTIL I FINISH UP AROUND HERE.

AFTER THAT, I'LL SHOW YOU THE SOURCE OF MY PARENT'S POWER.

...

SATOU-SENSEI...?

ISE...?!

FINISH UP...?

OW. OW OW.

THAT'S RIGHT... POCHI...!

PO...
POCHI ...?
WHY... AREN'T YOU MOVING...?
SENSEI ...!
SENSEI ...!

PLEASE STOP!

SENSEI!

TAKAGI ...

The main characters File2:

AKIMI SHIMIZU

A little air-headed, innocent female student. Explosive and tone-deaf. She yearned for Tsuchiya, the biology teacher, and accepted his evil genes into herself. However, she did not become a Nosferatu, but a carrier. After that, she displays and commands absurd strength at night, and plays the part of manual labor for Kurou's group. Even though she is now a "carrier," she still adores Tsuchiya and hopes for a coexistence between humans and Nosferatu.

FUKAYA

The School nurse. She holds the power to instantly heal even the most serious wounds by merely touching the affected part. People line up outside the Nurse's Office just to experience her embrace therapy. She was the ringleader behind turning Nogi and the others who had lost the will to live into zombies. In order to save Akasaka, she took on the mortal wounds Akasaka received in the fight with Nogi's group, exhausting her powers and causing her to take on the form of a child.

MAO TOOYAMA

After sunset, she prevents students from staying behind within Yotsuji Academy's walls, where she resides for an unknown reason. The principal and others call her "Mao-sama." Also, because Kurou exactly resembles her deceased brother, Shirou, who she loved, she can't hide her embarrassment. Carrying the female Nosferatu Seed, she calls Lemec, the Nosferatu King, "Otou-sama*". She has Neferti as a familiar.

*"Lord Father."

SONOBE

When it was made impossible to revive the zombie teachers, she was brought in as the new math teacher. She spreads strong pheromones. A long time ago, her name was Nactis. Of all the Nosferatu, she is the only one who is not a descendant of Lemec's bloodline. Previously, she was able to be reborn from inside the body of males, and that is how she has survived so long. Since Tsuchiya is unable to kill humans, she is the most dangerous member of Yostuji Academy's faculty. She is aiming for Takagi, bearer of the Seed.

CHAPTER 45
WHEN THE WIND STOPPED

...HEY.
HEY, DID YOU HEAR SOMETHING JUST NOW?
WHAT?
WHAT, ARE YOU PLAYING DUMB?
IF I CAN HEAR IT, YOU MOST CERTAINLY CAN HEAR IT TOO.
YOU SHOULD HAVE HEARD THAT CRYING VOICE!

SOMEHOW, IT RESEMBLES KUROU-CHAN'S VOICE...
HAS HE COME HERE TONIGHT...?
Just like Amano said...

I SWEAR... CAN'T HE KEEP IT QUIET WHEN HE'S ON THE HUNT?
YOU HEARD IT, DIDN'T YOU? SOMEBODY'S VOICE!
I don't hate screams, but...
phew.

THAT WAS TAKAGI'S VOICE.
I HEARD, "SENSEI, PLEASE STOP!"
HMPF.
MAX

↑ Honest.

HONEST.

AKASAKA.
AKASAKA.
RUSH

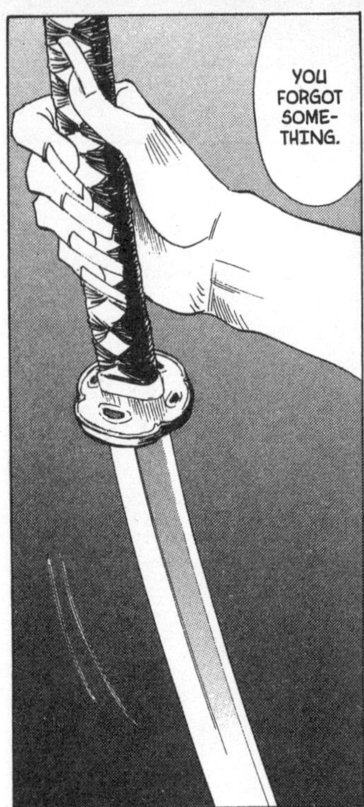
YOU FORGOT SOME-THING.

YOU'RE NOT A CARRIER. WITHOUT THIS, YOU'D BE EATEN JUST LIKE THAT.
AH... THANKS ...

DON'T SLASH REPEA-TEDLY.
?

STAB.

THAT WILL PROBABLY BE MORE EFFECTIVE AGAINST NOSFERATU.

WH... WHY?

IS IT OKAY? AREN'T THEY FAMILY?

I DON'T CARE.
I JUST WANT TO KNOW THAT KATANA'S POWER.

THE WOUND I RECEIVED STILL HASN'T CLOSED.

WHO ATTACKED KUROU-CHAN? I FORGOT TO ASK ...

... NOSFE-RATU...
THEY DON'T FOLLOW THEIR OWN FAMILY...
ALWAYS ALONE...
AND THAT'S FINE...

WHERE ARE YOU, KUROU-CHAN?
I HEARD YOUR VOICE, SO YOU SHOULDN'T BE FAR...
SEN-SEI...
!
WHAM
PL... PLEASE WAIT A SECOND!
SENSEI!
SENSEI! ISE IS...
SENSEI!

BADUMP
SATOU...
BADUMP
WHAT DID YOU DO TO ISE...?
NO...
I HAVE TO CLEAR MY HEAD!
SA ...
PITA
PITA
SA...
SATOU!

IF YOU DON'T RELEASE HIM RIGHT NOW...

OOF!

STAGGER

STEP ASIDE!

Akasaka?!

AHH!

AHH!

HE'S ALREADY STABBED?!

WHA?

AKASAKA-SAN?

I KNOW YOU CAME TO SCHOOL, BUT WHEN DID YOU...

You managed to pierce right through my middle with one stroke...

EVEN THOUGH I STABBED HIM...
BADUMP
BADUMP
WAS IT NOT EFFECTIVE ...?
THIS SWORD IS ...

AKASAKA-SAN, WHERE DID YOU GET THIS SWORD...?
PITA
PITA
PITA
すたたたっ

ESCAPE IS IMPOSSIBLE ...

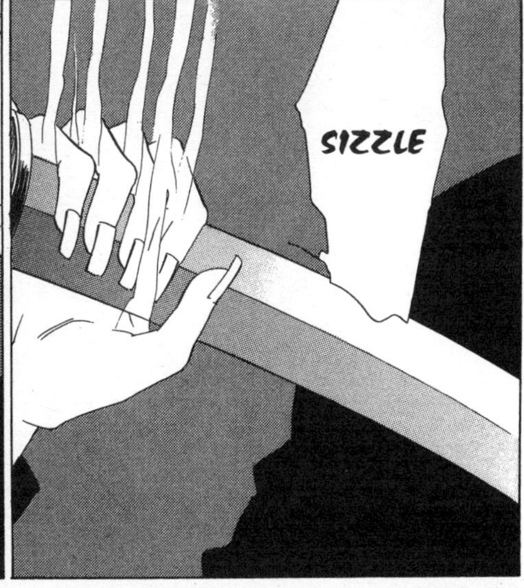
SIZZLE

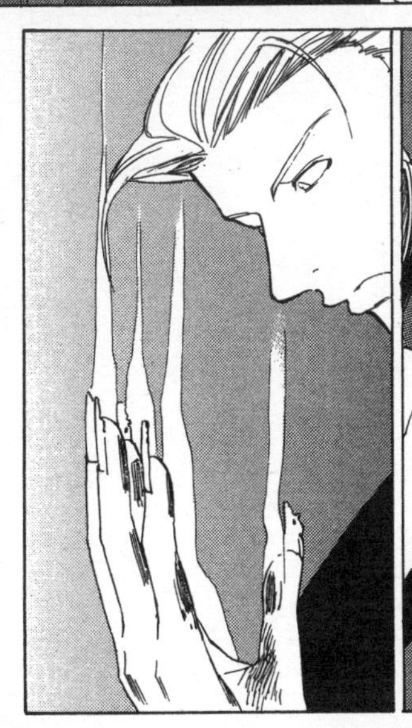

HEY, ARE YOU... ARE YOU OKAY?

HAH.

SATOU IS COMING! HE'LL FIND US FOR SURE!

HAH.

IS EVERYONE ELSE NOT HERE? YOSHIKUNI AND THE OTHERS...

WHAT WAS THAT BLOOD ON SATOU?!
WERE YOU BITTEN? ARE YOU OKAY?!
... AKASAKA ...

I'M SURPRISED ...
I DIDN'T THINK TO SEE YOU AT SCHOOL ...

EH? ME?!
YEAH... WELL... UMM...

WHY ARE YOU HERE?!
HERE OF ALL PLACES...?!

...KUROU-CHAN ... YOU WERE ATTACKED...

AKASAKA, YOU IDIOT!

Wah.

RIGHT, RIGHT.
YOU'RE NOT A CARRIER, AKASAKA!
THIS SCHOOL ISN'T COMPLETELY SAFE YET!
So cute...
THAT'S RIGHT.

↑ Not listening.

AND... I CAN'T RELY ON POCHI... ANYMORE...
I CAN'T... PROTECT ANYONE RIGHT NOW...
POCHI?
I'LL PROTECT YOU, KUROU-CHAN...
Gaha...
What's a Pochi?
Oh my final fantasy!

On a whole different planet ↑

WHY DID YOU DIE AND DISAPPEAR ON ME?!

WAAAH!

KUROU-CHAN... CA... CALM DOWN ...

BE... BE QUIET...

UWAH.

FOOTSTEPS ...

SOME-ONE'S COMING ...

STOP

...

I DEFINITELY HEARD TWO VOICES...

AND SPEAKING OF WHICH, TAKAGI'S BAWLS...

HOWEVER, I DON'T SMELL HUMANS...

!
ビリッ
SHOCK

SHH
SHH
RATTLE
RATTLE

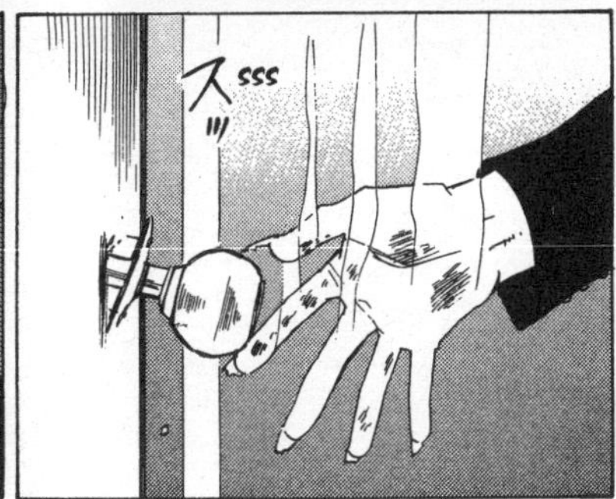
スッ
SSS

...
SILENCE

PLEASE COME OUT,
YOU TWO.

?

IT'S THE SAME AS THAT NIGHT...

WHEN TAKAGI-KUN LEFT THE COFFIN...

THE PRESENCE OF KUROU TAKAGI IS IN THIS ROOM...

I CAN'T SNIFF OUT TAKAGI-KUN'S LOCATION...

EVEN THOUGH HE'S NEARBY, WE'RE NOT AFFECTED...
NEITHER THE "RED ANGEL" NOR MYSELF...

AND EARLIER HE BROKE INTO MY TERRITORY TOO EASILY...
And I can't break into his...
IS THIS PROOF OF THE MAN WHO WILL BECOME THE KING OF THE NOSFERATU?

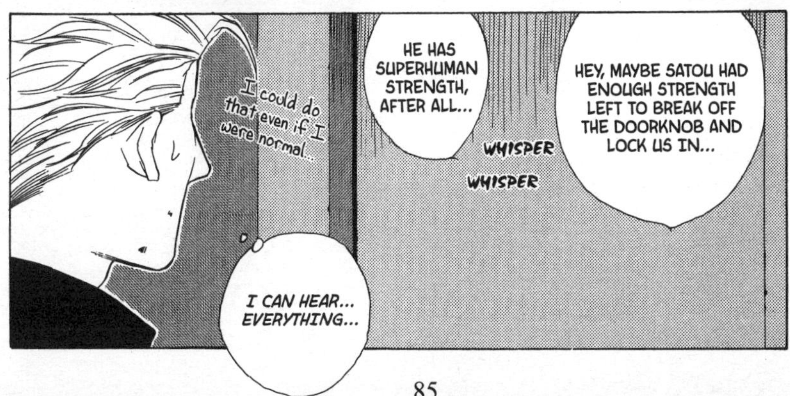
HEY, MAYBE SATOU HAD ENOUGH STRENGTH LEFT TO BREAK OFF THE DOORKNOB AND LOCK US IN...
HE HAS SUPERHUMAN STRENGTH, AFTER ALL...
WHISPER
WHISPER
I could do that even if I were normal...
I CAN HEAR... EVERYTHING...

LET'S LOOK AT THE STATE OF THINGS TONIGHT...

I DIDN'T THINK CAPTURING THE SEED WOULD BE THIS TROUBLE-SOME...

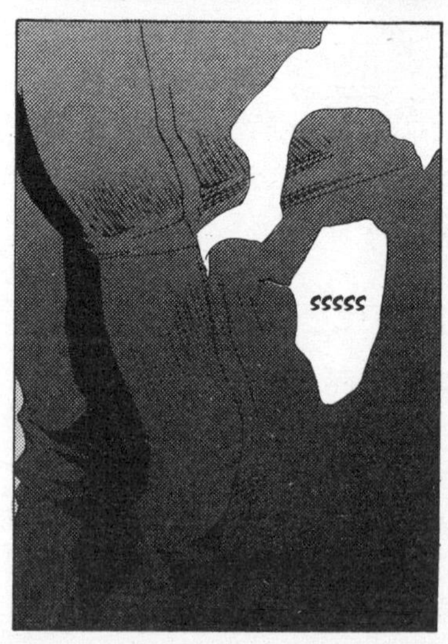

SSSSS

LOOKS LIKE HE LEFT...
I'M NOT QUITE SURE, BUT I THINK WE'RE SAFE ...

AKA-SAKA...
WHAT?
I'M GLAD YOU'RE ALL BETTER.
A lot happened, but...
WELCOME BACK.
WAH!
BUMP
SQUEEZE

BUT AKASAKA, A LOT OF YOUR LIMBS REALLY WERE BROKEN, HUH?
I thought you looked manly.
BADUMP
WHOOSH
GRAB
S...
SORRY.
All things considered, I think I recovered quickly...

BUT... REALLY...
I'M SORRY FOR A LOT OF THINGS... I JUST WANTED TO SAY IT AT LEAST ONCE.

SNIFFLE
Not listening!
KUROU-CHAN?

POCHI IS...

WHAT HAPPENED?
I DON'T KNOW...
WHEN I SAW HIM EARLIER, HE WASN'T MOVING...

SHOULD WE BRING HIM TO A DOCTOR?!
A VET?!
A PEDIATRICIAN?
A DENTIST?!
CA... CALM DOWN, KUROU-CHAN!

GEEZ, WHAT'S UP?
HE LOOKS DEAD...

POCHI... AND ISE...
ISE?!
WHY DID THESE THINGS HAPPEN...?
DID SOMETHING HAPPEN?

TWITCH

ISE...!
WHERE IS TETSUZOU AT THIS HOUR? WHAT IS HE UP TO...?
He's been a little cruel lately, fooling around at night...
HE'S NOT HOME...
I THOUGHT HE MIGHT BE HERE AT THE HOSPITAL...

I THOUGHT I'D AT LEAST SEE HIS FACE WHEN I GOT HOME ...

YOU'VE LOVED RABBITS SINCE YOU WERE SMALL, HUH, TSUGIKO...

IT'S SO OLD, BUT IT SENDS A MESSAGE...

IT'S BEEN PASSED BACK AND FORTH BETWEEN THE TWINS SO MANY TIMES ...

MOM...

TSU... TSUGIKO!

DID I WAKE YOU ...?!

NO...

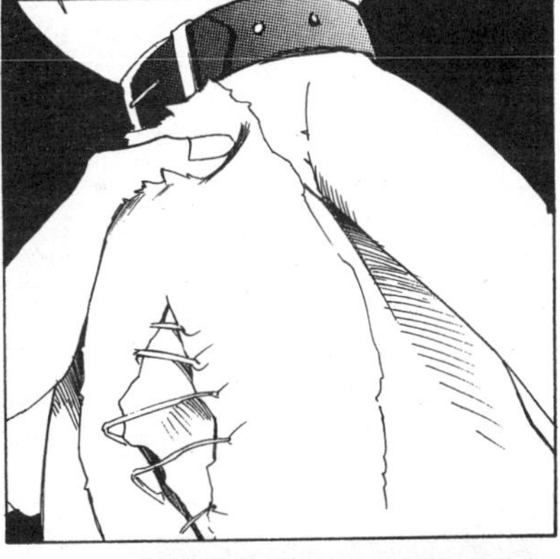

WH... WHAT DO YOU MEAN?

THIS...!

倫子へ

TO NORIKO

WHY DO YOU HAVE THIS, TSUGIKO...?!

DID...
DID HE THINK THIS WOULD SCARE ME... ?!
RIP
RIP

SCARE ...?

WHY DIDN'T YOU TELL ME ANYTHING?!
TSUGIKO ...?!

I SAID I DON'T KNOW ANYTHING!
AREN'T YOU THE ONE WHO'S HIDING THINGS FROM ME...?!

...

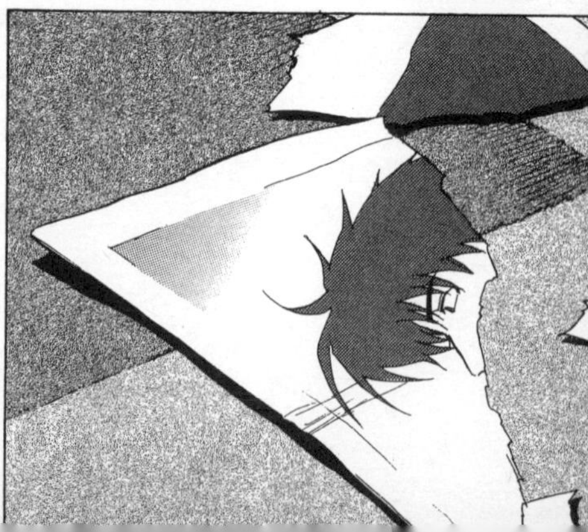

IT'S KUROU!

KUROU? THE PERSON YOU'RE ALWAYS TALKING ABOUT, POCHI?
IT HAS NOTHING TO DO WITH TAKAGI. THAT LOOKS LIKE A FAIRLY OLD PHOTO.
IT'S THE SAME FACE!
HMM...
SAME FACE, YOU SAY?
HE HAS A MUCH NICER PERSONALITY AND FACE THAN TETSUZOU! I RECOMMEND HIM!
DON'T FREELY RECOMMEND PEOPLE TO MY SISTER!
KUROU... TAKAGI...

The main characters File 3:

TSUCHIYA

An evil teacher with an intense smell of danger lingering about him. Popular among the entire female student population. The perpetrator who killed Okamoto. Skilled with his hands, he's in charge of repairing the broken zombie teachers. His name as a Nosferatu is John Garous, and he inherited his evil genes from Loups Garous. As the last disciple of the Nosferatu, he lives faithful to his instincts. However, because of Kurou, he is forbidden from killing any humans at present.

LOUPS GAROUS

Tsuchiya's (John Garous's) Nosferatu parent. She eats the entrails of still-living humans and then assumes their form. Still regenerating her body from damage incurred from the "Nosferatu Hunt" in the 80's, she currently resides in the "Grave of the Nosferatu." Loups looked past Tsuchiya and saw a gifted individual who could become a Nosferatu, and thus she infected him with her evil genes. Since she finds her son to be so cute, she's a bit of a doting mother.

SATOU

A language teacher at Yotsuji Academy, he's the only one who has common sense where all the other teachers lack it. His parent is the "Red Angel," the divine power of the vampire Nosferatu. For some reason, he seems to have the self-control to stay his hand against the student population. Moreover, he's strong enough to inflict mortal (?) wounds on Tsuchiya. He had only created one member in the next generation of Nosferatu when he injected his evil genes into Ise...

RED ANGEL (AKA NO TENSHI)

Satou's parent, the divine power of the vampire Nosferatu who possesses colossal energy. Plans the revival of the vampire clan. Moreover, much like Loups, clashed with Carriers during the "Nosferatu Hunt" in the 80's and lost a bit of power, but still possesses great strength. In order to retrieve the Nosferatu Seed from Takagi in the Coffin of Oblivion, the Red Angel passed its power down to Satou in order to trick Ise into being Takagi's substitute in the coffin.

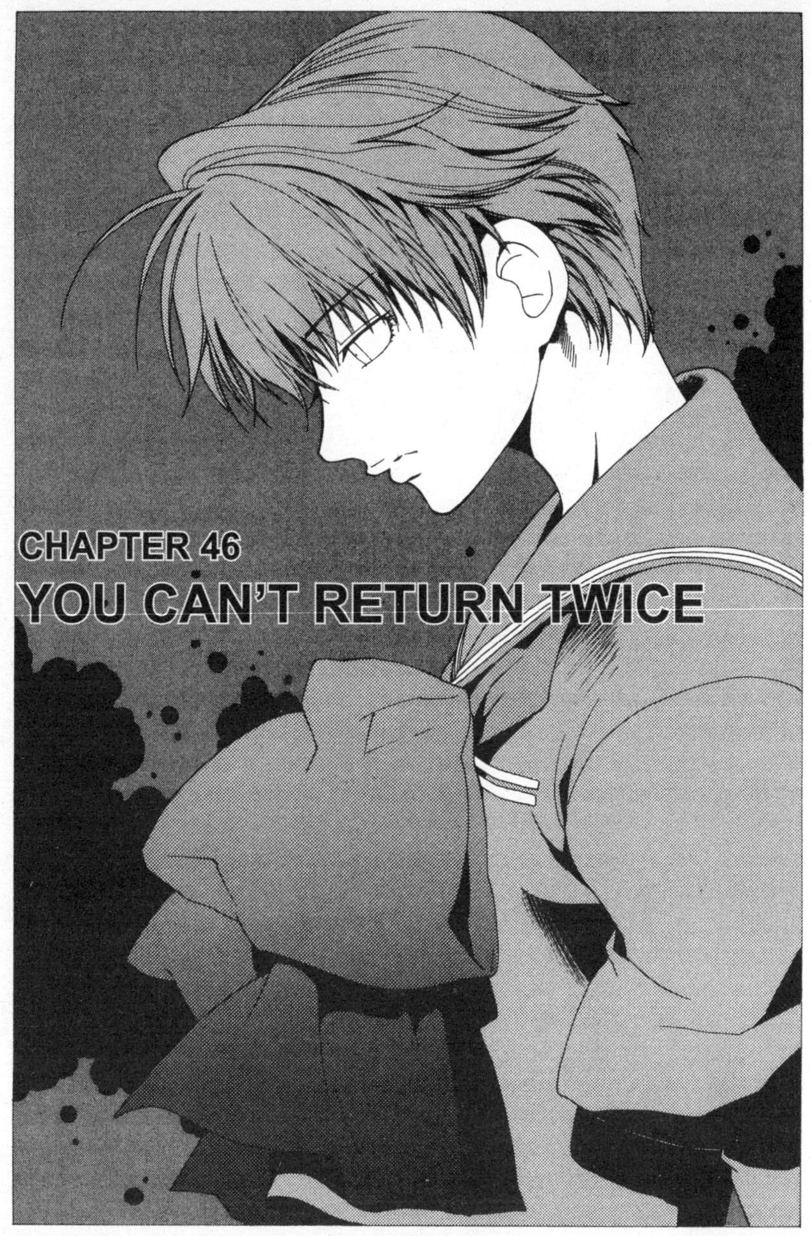
CHAPTER 46
YOU CAN'T RETURN TWICE

THE DAWN WILL BREAK SOON.
IT WILL BE USELESS THIS TIME, WON'T IT?
MAO-SAMA... THE WAY YOU ARE RIGHT NOW, YOU WILL CONTINUE TO WANDER AROUND LOST.
NOTHING WILL BE ACCOMPL-ISHED.

NOTHING...? AND IF I USE THE KEY...?
WHAT IN THE WORLD WILL...?

HA HA.
THIS SCHOOL DOESN'T MEAN ANYTHING YET.
IT HAS NOT TRULY AWAKENED.

WE NOSFERATU GATHER HERE FOR THAT PURPOSE...
WE GATHER MINORS AT THIS PLACE CALLED A "SCHOOL."

IT DOESN'T MATTER IF WE INSTEAD CALL THOSE MINORS GIFTED INDIVIDUALS.
THIS KEY ...
THIS KEY ...!

THIS KEY WAS INSIDE MY BROTHER'S URN...!

AND... MY DEAD BROTHER'S BONES THAT SHOULD HAVE BEEN LEFT FROM THE CREMATION

WERE NOT IN HIS GRAVE!

DID YOU ATTEND YOUR BROTHER'S CREMATION?
NO, YOU DID NOT SEE IT.

CIRCUMSTANCES DID NOT ALLOW YOU TO GO TO YOUR MOTHER'S AND BROTHER'S FUNERALS, RIGHT?
IS EVERY-THING THAT'S HAPPENING NOW RELATED TO MY BROTHER?
QUIVER

MY BROTHER, SHIROU ...

HE DIED IN FRONT OF MY EYES...!

YOU SHOULD UNDERSTAND EVEN IF I SAY NOTHING.

HE POSSESSED A NOSFERATU SEED...

EVEN THOUGH YOU GRADUALLY BEGAN TO ACCEPT YOUR BROTHER'S DEATH...

EVEN THOUGH YOU GRADUALLY BEGAN TO THINK ABOUT NORMAL PEOPLE...

MAO...

THIS IS FINE...

I AM BEING REBORN...
MOM IS GOING WITH ME...
I'M... HAPPY...
EVEN IF WE CAN'T LIVE TOGETHER.
LET'S GO, SHIROU.
I CAN ONLY SEE YOU.

THUD

WHOOSH

WHY...

MOM...

BROTHER...

WHY DIDN'T YOU CHOOSE ME...?

Huh?

JOLT
KUROU-CHA...
NOT HERE ...

DON'T GO AND LEAVE ME ALONE WITH A CORPSE!
Look over here!
Look over here!

...
WHERE DID YOU GO BY YOURSELF...?
PHEW
After noticing the corpse, feels lonely after crying by herself.
KUROU-CHAN...
Dammit!
BANG BANG
THE TWO OF US WERE ALONE TOGETHER, AND I CARELESSLY FELL ASLEEP! I'M AN IDIOT IDIOT IDIOT IDIOT!
THUMP THUMP
FOR MISSING OUT ON HIS CHANCE TO CONFESS, I'M SUCH AN IDIOT IDIOT IDIOT ...
Hippo
SINCE IT'S TURNED LIGHT OUT, IS THE DANGER GONE?
HAH. HAH.
...huh?

I FEEL STRANGELY RELAXED.
I WONDER WHY.
I'M WORRIED ABOUT POCHI, BUT...
MORE IMPORTANTLY ...

OF COURSE...
I HAVE TO SEE...

ISE...
ISE...?!
DI... DID SOMEBODY MOVE HIM?! OR ELSE...
YOU'RE AWFULLY LOUD FOR SO EARLY IN THE MORNING!

BE QUIET.

MY HEAD HURTS...

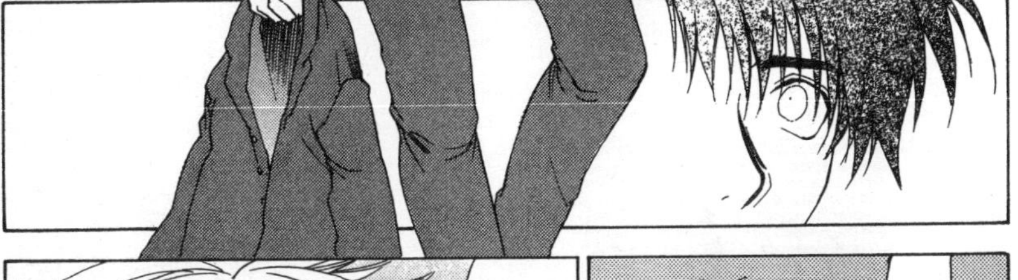

TAKAGI ...
TELL ME...
WHAT AM I...?
...!
IS MY ...
FACE PALE...?
ARE MY EYES BLANK...?
AHH!
YOUR FACE HAS NO COMPLEXION, AND YOUR EYES HAVE NO FOCUS!
SHOUTING WITHOUT THINKING.
SERIOUSLY... HOW ANNOYING...

THAT'S IMPOSS-IBLE!

I'M GOING TO STRANGLE YOU TO DEATH, YOU BIG IDIOT!

GET MAD ALL YOU WANT, BUT IT WON'T CHANGE REALITY, ISE.

...

...I THOUGHT DEATH... WOULD BE... MORE...

SLUGGISH

...I KINDA FEEL LIKE SOMETHING IS PAUSED...

IF THIS IS DEATH...

...IT'S NOT SUCH A BIG DEAL...

Haha.

YOU... YOU DON'T NORMALLY TURN INTO A ZOMBIE ...

TELL ME.

YOU SHOULD HAVE SEEN IT.

WH... WHY DO YOU WANT TO KNOW ABOUT THAT...?

THE MOMENT SATOU KILLED ME...!
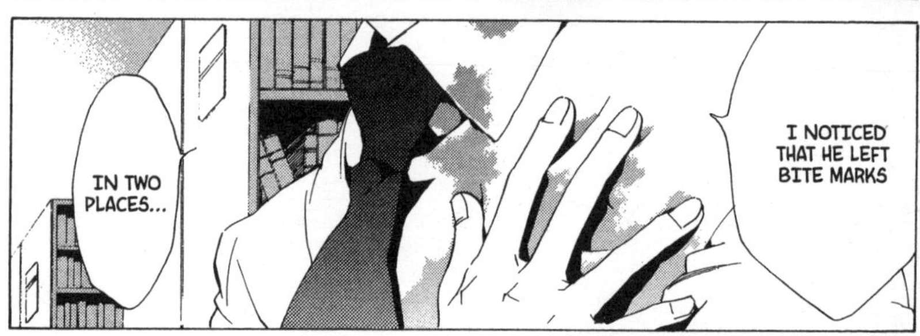
I NOTICED THAT HE LEFT BITE MARKS
IN TWO PLACES...

DOESN'T IT HURT...?
IT DOESN'T HURT... BUT I FEEL SOMEHOW LIGHTER ON MY FEET...
AND THE WOUNDS FEEL HOT ...

AND MY ENTIRE BODY FEELS CHILLY...
AND MY FINGERTIPS' SENSES ARE DULLED...
Ahh, you're really a zombie! Ise! Ise!

WELL, ANYWAY, I'M LEAVING...
WHERE ARE YOU GOING??
I've decided.
HOME.

I'M GOING... HOME...

I HAVE FUTURE PLANS FOR THIS BODY...

NORIKO ...

Zombies can't go home, Ise-kun...

IF I DON'T... CONSULT HER...

ISE!

ARE YOU OK?!

STRANGE THAT I ASK, BUT ARE YOU OK?!

ANYWAY, LET'S TAKE HIM TO THE NURSE'S OFFICE.

I'M SORRY, TAKAGI-KUN...
DRAG
DRAG
DRAG
AREN'T YOU ANGRY, FUKAYA-SENSEI...?

WHY?
WE'RE TROUBLESOME. EVEN THOUGH THEY SAID NOT TO COME TO SCHOOL, WE STILL CAME...
ON TOP OF THAT, I'M ONLY GOOD FOR PROTECTING MY FRIENDS... AND I CAN'T EVEN DO THAT...

YOU'RE TROUBLESOME FOR MORE THAN JUST THAT, TAKAGI-KUN.

BECAUSE YOU HAVE THE NOSFERATU SEED.
I... I DON'T FULLY UNDERSTAND, BUT THE SEED LETS ME BECOME THE KING OF THE NOSFERATU... SO WHY...

SLIP

I...

ISE ...?!

RUMBLE

THE GATES OPENED, HUH? I WONDER IF TAKAGI-KUN AND ISETCHI WILL RETURN SOON...

WE WENT FROM THE TAKEOVER OF YOTSUJI ACADEMY TO NOT SLEEPING AND IT BECOMING MORNING...

IN ANY CASE, I THINK IT REALLY BENEFITS US THAT AKIMI HELPED OUT TOUYAMA.

Yawn...

TOUYAMA...? IS SHE PART OF THE STRATEGY?

BAM

TOUYAMA...?

WHAT THE HELL? WHAT'S WITH YOUR LISTLESS TONE?

IT'S UP TO YOU TO GET HER INVOLVED.

...I PROBABLY CAN'T.

BUT YOU'RE ALWAYS SAYING STUFF LIKE, "I'LL PERSUADE HER!"

Ahaha.

...I DON'T THINK THE DAY WILL EVER COME WHEN TOUYAMA WILL NOTICE ME...
I GET THE FEELING SHE NEVER LOOKS AT ME.

A RARE MOMENT OF WEAKNESS ...
Sorry.
THERE'S THE MATTER OF TOUYAMA'S DEAD BROTHER.

WHETHER ASLEEP OR AWAKE, HE'S THE ONLY THING SHE EVER THINKS ABOUT.
BUT HE'S DEAD, ISN'T HE?!
What the hell.
FURTHERMORE, AREN'T THEY SIBLINGS?

I HAD NO IDEA...
AH, FORBIDDEN LOVE...
SHE'S DEFINITELY STRANGE...
TO THINK TOUYAMA-SAN HAD SUCH AN ABNORMAL LOVE AFFAIR...
TOUYAMA PROBABLY WON'T SPEAK TO YOU EITHER.

IS IT WRONG TO LOVE A TEACHER?
HE'S NOT A NORMAL TEACHER!
ALL YOU CARE ABOUT ARE PRETTY HIPS, NISHI-WAKI-KUN!
Kya! Kya! Forbidden love!
YOU'RE WRONG!
Completely wrong!
I could jump in a spring and they wouldn't notice.

UGHHH...

I HATE YOU, NISHI-WAKI-KUN!

DON'T SAY STRANGE THINGS!

WHO'S BEING... SO LOUD...?

FIRST OF ALL ...

DID I SPEND THE ENTIRE NIGHT MAKING FRIENDS WITH YOU GUYS?

I PROBABLY WON'T BE COMING BACK TO THIS SCHOOL.

I ALREADY SENT NOTIFIC-ATION OF MY MOVING.
A horrible reason!
Already proceeded with the formalities...

UMM... KIKUCHI-SAN... WHY?
WHY ARE YOU QUITTING YOTSUJI ACADEMY?

THE CURRICULUM DOESN'T SEEM TO SUIT ME.
FOR SOME REASON... I DON'T LIKE THE BUILDINGS OR THE CAMPUS...
AND ALSO...

I DON'T HAVE ANY FRIENDS HERE.

...

SHE DIDN'T... HAVE ANY FRIENDS...

THAT'S NOT TRUE... THE TWO FRIENDS SHE HAD BOTH DIED.

DOES SHE NOT REMEMBER THEM ANYMORE ...?
YEAH...
SEEMS LIKE IT...

AKIMI THOUGHT THE SAME THING.
WHEN THE PRINCIPAL ERASED KIKUCHI-SAN'S MEMORIES...
AKASAKA, WHO GOT INVOLVED FROM PURSUING OKAMOTO...
AND US AS WELL ...

WE CAN TAKE THAT PATH AND LEAVE THE SCHOOL BEHIND...

WELCOME BACK!

ISETCHI!

Character File Special:Ise Family 1

TETSUZOU ISE

Moving at his own pace, he often goes out alone. He was dating the black-haired student Mari Kobayashi, but in reality it seemed like she was not the only one. In order to save his older sister, Tsugiko, he attempted to turn himself into a Nosferatu by approaching Satou. However, he was instead used as Takagi's replacement in the "coffin" and came close to death.

TSUGIKO ISE

Being hospitalized for leukemia, she is Tetsuzou's older twin sister. In middle school, the siblings formed a musical duo. In charge of vocals and lyrics, her musical talent was extraordinary. After she was hospitalized during the fall of her third year of middle school, she underwent various treatments, but she was never cured. She had planned to attend Yotsuji Academy along with Tetsuzou...

CHAPTER 47
DAYLIGHT FEVER

I...

ISE ...?!

AHH!

You can't support your classmate who is on top of you and strangling your neck.

I...

MM-PH!

STOMP

I'M GOING HOME...

ISE, WAIT!

ISE!

...

PITA

PITA

Manga's hero.

YOU SAY YOU'RE GOING HOME,

BUT IF YOU TRY AND LEAVE THOSE GATES...

Oh, hey!

Hey, you!

CRACK

DO YOU NOT REMEMBER ME...?
THE FIRST NIGHT WE WERE HERE, SATOU-SENSEI HELPED US ESCAPE OUTSIDE...
OW.

PLEASE GO, TAKAGI-KUN.

PEOPLE WITH EVIL GENES CAN'T LEAVE THE SCHOOL...!
IF HE TRIES WITH NO AVAIL TO LEAVE THE SCHOOL...
WELCOME BACK!
ISETCHI!
Man, looks like you ran into trouble.
GEEZ, WHAT ARE YOU DOING...?

HM?
...

TA... TAKAGI-KUN...?
WAIT!
TAP
TAP
TAP
TAP
ISE!
YEP.

I DEFINITELY WON'T LET YOU GO OUTSIDE!
WHOOSH
っぱ

...

WHAT DO YOU PLAN TO DO, TAKAGI...?

Looks painful.

LIVELY, AREN'T THEY?

WOBBLE
WOBBLE

IT'S RARE TO SEE ISETCHI LOOK SO DANGEROUS.
YOU'RE SO HAPPY, YOUR NOSE IS BLEEDING.

IF I DON'T MAKE SURE...
WIPE
WHAT'S HAPPENING INSIDE OF ISE'S BODY?

JOHN!
SLIDE
JOHN GAROUS!

DON'T CALL FOR ME.

I DON'T HAVE MUCH FREE TIME.

LEND ME A HAND!

I CAN'T CARRY HIM.

HEH.

"PAIN."

SOON HE'LL PASS OUT FROM IT.

IT'S BEEN A LONG TIME SINCE I TASTED IT AS WELL.

DO YOU FIND IT HARD TO BELIEVE? THAT NOSFERATU FEEL PAIN?

WELL, NURSE?

THIS IS ISE'S HOUSE...

WHAT AM I DOING...?

I CAN'T KEEP STANDING GUARD HERE...

IF I FIND ANYTHING OUT, IT'LL BE AT SUNSET.
BUT I CAN AT LEAST WAIT UNTIL NIGHT.

A while back, my child couldn't stop staring at a middle-school student.
My husband did the same thing with a beautiful office worker.
STARE

I MUST MERELY SEEM LIKE A HIGH-SCHOOL STUDENT WHO IS DITCHING CLASS AND LOITERING.

KYA!
KYA!
IT'S PEACEFUL OUT.
Yawn.

...!

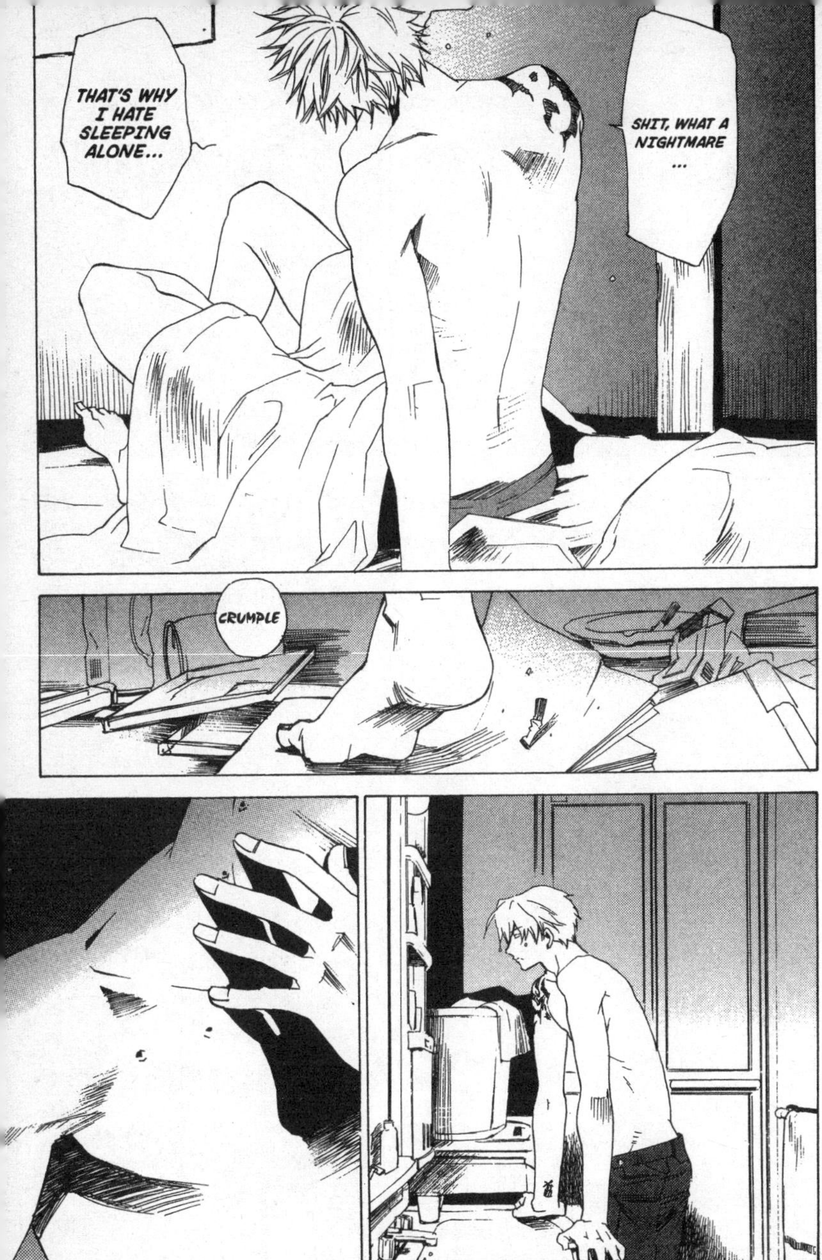

SHIT, WHAT A NIGHTMARE ...

THAT'S WHY I HATE SLEEPING ALONE...

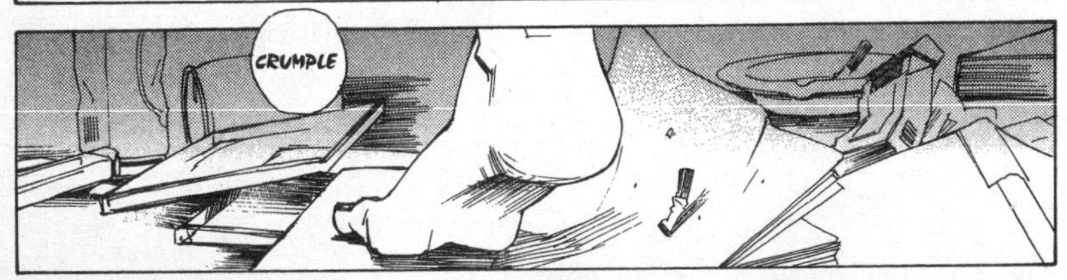

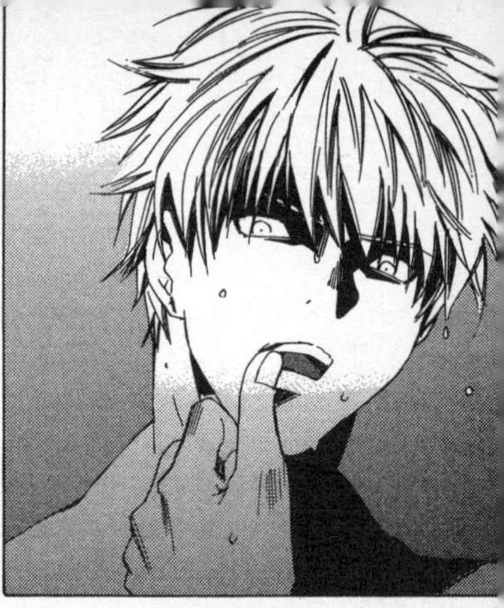

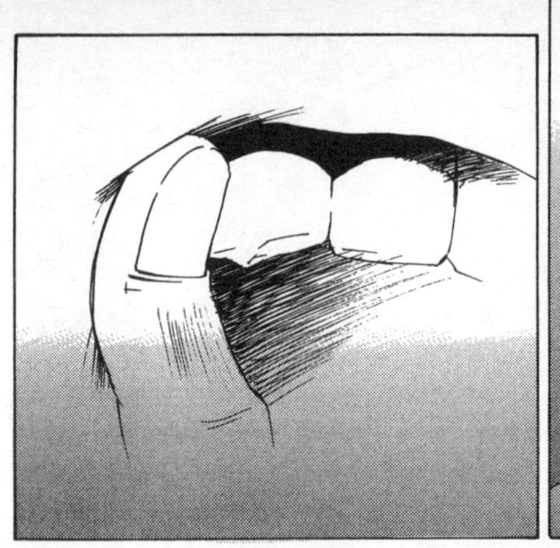

HE CAME OUT...
HE'S NOT IN UNIFORM ...

I WONDER IF HE PLANS TO RETURN TO SCHOOL...
OR ELSE...

IT SURE IS PACKED AT NIGHT.

THIS IS MY FIRST TIME RIDING THIS LINE.

HM?

PSHHHH
GATHUNK

AH!
I'M GETTING OFF! I'M GETTING OFF!

I WONDER WHERE HE'S GOING.
Heh heh.
I WONDER IF THIS IS WHAT HE NORMALLY DOES OUTSIDE.
WHISPER
Disgusting.

WHERE HAVE I SEEN SAILOR OUTFITS BEFORE?
Yay yay!
They're only girls.

...
Who?
Mari's boyfriend?
Oooh, show me!
TECCHAN!

Ohh.
SOMEONE LEFT HICKIES ON MY TETSUZOU?
MARI?

AH... IF WE COULDN'T MEET, I WOULD TRY AND MAKE A CLEAN CUT AND FORGET YOU.
Hehehe.
I DON'T KNOW WHO THE WOMAN IS, BUT I'LL CURSE AND KILL HER.
What are you waiting for?
PL... PLEASE...

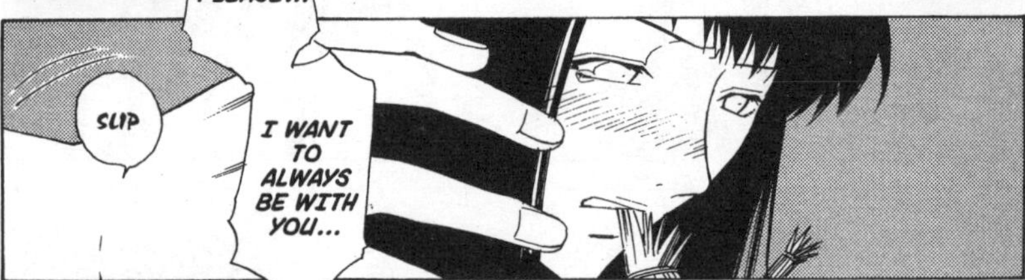
I WANT TO ALWAYS BE WITH YOU...
SLIP

YOU'RE IMPOS-SIBLE ...

TECC-HAN ...

AH, I'M BASICALLY A PEEPING TOM...
WOBBLE

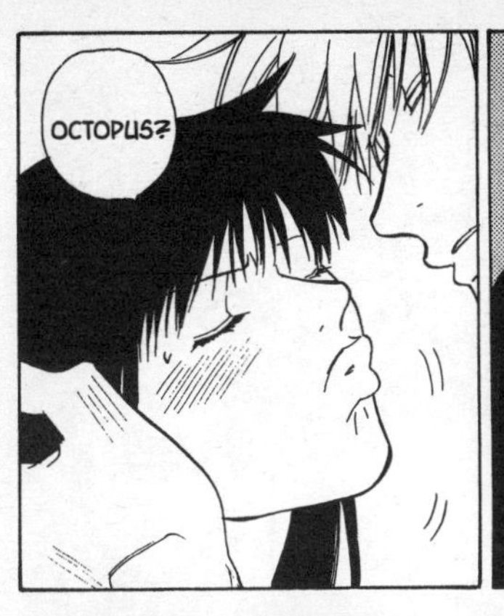

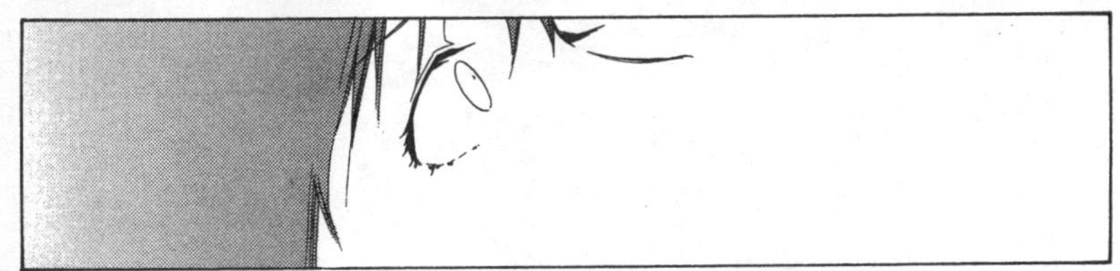

...!

CHOMP

OW ...!
THAT HURTS!
OW...

OW...
ISE!
NO...!
SHOVE

TAKAGI!

WHAT ARE YOU DOING?
YOU WERE REALLY BITING ME JUST NOW...
TAKAGI!
WHAT IS THIS?!
EXPLAIN YOURSELF!

ARE YOU OK? THAT GIRL'S PROBABLY ANGRY AT YOU.
NO MATTER HOW ANGRY SHE IS, I DON'T LOVE HER.

...YOU REALIZED I WAS TAILING YOU...?
YOU'RE BECOMING A FIRST-CLASS STALKER, TAKAGI.
You don't wait in front of someone's house for that long.

MAYBE YOU WERE REALLY PLANNING ON EATING THAT GIRL...
I WAS JUST MAKING SURE!

I THOUGHT MAYBE I HAD BECOME A NOSFERATU...
EVEN THOUGH IT'S NIGHT, I HAVEN'T SEEMED TO HAVE GROWN FANGS.

STILL, I DON'T KNOW WHAT I AM.
SO TELL ME EVERYTHING THAT HAPPENED TO ME LAST NIGHT.

STOP...!
RUN AWAY, ISE...!
ISE...!
...!
THIS IS...?
BUBBLE
BUBBLE

THE BITE HEALED...? THAT'S WHY HE BIT ME A SECOND TIME...

AND THEN?

THEN IT WAS OVER.

OVER?
YOU'RE GONNA DIE.
DIE.
Stop cursing me.
PHEW
GOT IT? THIS IS IMPORTANT!
WAS IT REALLY A SIMPLE BITE? OR ELSE HE WOULD HAVE STUCK LIKE A LEECH.

AT THAT TIME, SATOU HAD BEEN PLANNING ON KILLING ME.
AH, NO.
AFTER BITING YOU THE SECOND TIME, HE RELEASED YOU.

HE LEFT YOU THERE ON THE FLOOR, GRABBED ME, AND LEFT THE LIBRARY.

BECAUSE YOU WERE LEFT WITH A LOT OF BLOOD LOSS, I THOUGHT YOU MIGHT HAVE DIED...

WELL, YOU CAN SEE I'M NOT DEAD.

BUT NO ONE SEEMS TO KNOW WHETHER I'M A ZOMBIE, NOSFERATU, OR SOMETHING ELSE.

What are you, really?

BUT YOU LEFT SCHOOL JUST FINE...

BUT WHY DID THE BITES HEAL? AND WHY DIDN'T HE COMPLETELY EAT ME?
Hah...
IT'S NOT LIKE IT WAS TOOTH DECAY...!
THAT IDIOT! YOU DON'T SINK ROTTING TEETH INTO SOMEONE ELSE'S BODY!
CRINKLE
CRINKLE
CRINKLE
IT'S NOT LIKE IT WAS TOOTH DECAY...!
TELL ME WHAT I'VE BECOME!
YOU IDIOT!
YOU IDIOT!
You sure are hitting a lot of things today... myself included...
HE'S NOT A ZOMBIE, AND HE'S NOT A NOSFERATU, BUT ISE DOES... SEEM SUPER-HUMAN...

...
THAT'S HOW YOU STOP THE PAIN...
WE'LL HAVE TO CUT YOUR CHEST OFF TOO.
THUD
THUD

RATHER THAN THE WOUND HEALING, THE EVIL GENES ARE BURNING OFF BIT BY BIT.

THAT IS THE POWER OF A CARRIER...

MORE ACCURATELY, THAT IS THE POWER OF THE SWORD THAT HAS THE POWERS OF A CARRIER.

TO US NOSFERATU, WHO DON'T HAVE NORMAL FATES, "PAIN" IS A DANGEROUS SIGN.
ONLY CARRIERS CAN GIVE THAT TO US.

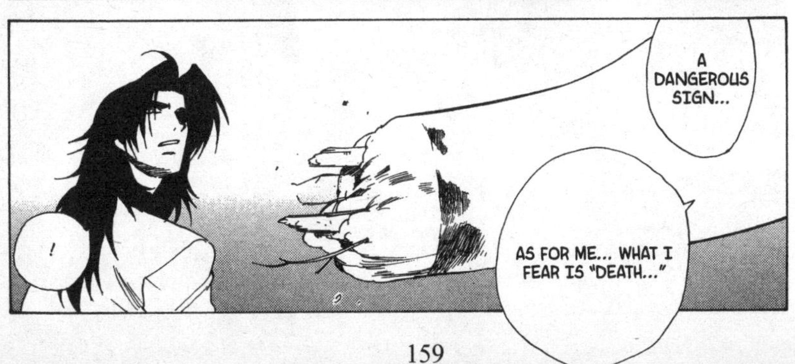

A DANGEROUS SIGN...
AS FOR ME... WHAT I FEAR IS "DEATH..."
!

IMPOSSIBLE!
HE'S ALREADY STARTED REGENERATING...?
IT'S THANKS TO THE LITTLE BIT OF SPECIAL BLOOD I DRANK LAST NIGHT.
SPECIAL BLOOD, YOU SAY?
THE POWER IS OVERFLOWING THROUGH MY BODY...

I PLAN TO HAVE A TALK WITH HIM

ABOUT TETSUZOU ISE'S TRUE CHARACTER.

Character File Special:Ise Family 2

HIDEHISA MUROI

A member of the Nosferatu hunt in the 80's, he's a flame-wielding " Carrier." Around the time he joined a motorcycle gang, he met Noriko, a policewoman. He told Tetsuzou that he's his true father, even though he only appears to be twenty. Also, delivering meals to Tsuchiya, he seems to be cooperating with the Nosferatu. His suspicious activities stand out.

NORIKO ISE

He's been a little cruel lately, fooling around at night...

The somewhat delinquent mother of Tetsuzou and Tsugiko, aged thirty-five. Raising her kids as a single mother, her parenting technique involves a doctrine of non-intervention. A long time ago, she used to be a policewoman in the traffic division department, but now she works as an insurance salesperson. Separated from her husband (Muroi), she received a large sum of consolation money, but she does not spend it. For some reason, she refuses to bring up the subject of her husband.

CHAPTER 48
3KINGS

YOU DON'T NEED TO PASS.
CRUNCH
CRUNCH
CRUNCH
...
LOUPS GAROUS ...
EVEN THOUGH KUROU TAKAGI MEANS EVERYTHING TO US...
RUMBLE
RUMBLE
YOU VAMPIRES HAVE BEATEN US OTHER NOSFERATU TO THE DRAW AND HAVE MADE THE SEED YOUR OWN.
FOR YOUR GROSS MISTAKES, I SHOULD EAT YOUR ENTRAILS, BUT...

VAMPIRE GRADE NOSFERATU ARE SUITABLE.
WEAK NOSFERATU, MUCH LIKE CARRIERS, DO NOT HAVE THE QUALITIES TO LEAD THE FUTURE GENERATIONS.

Don't come any closer!
HAS LEMEC-SAMA NOT PROMISED US THE RESTORATION OF ALL NOSFERATU?
WHAT HE WISHES FOR IS A SUCCESSOR WITH STRONG EVIL GENES.

YOU SAY THAT A LOT, DON'T YOU, RED ANGEL?
I WOULD LIKE TO SEE A VAMPIRE WHO HAS THE CHARISMA TO SUCCEED.

STOP IT, YOU TWO.
PRINC-IPAL...!

OUR ENTIRE POPULATION
HAS ALREADY BEEN REDUCED TO BE WEAKER THAN HUMANS.

LEMEC-SAMA HAS ALREADY THOUGHT OF A WAY TO SAVE OUR WEAK PEOPLE.

NOW THEN, COME WITH ME, SATOU-SENSEI.

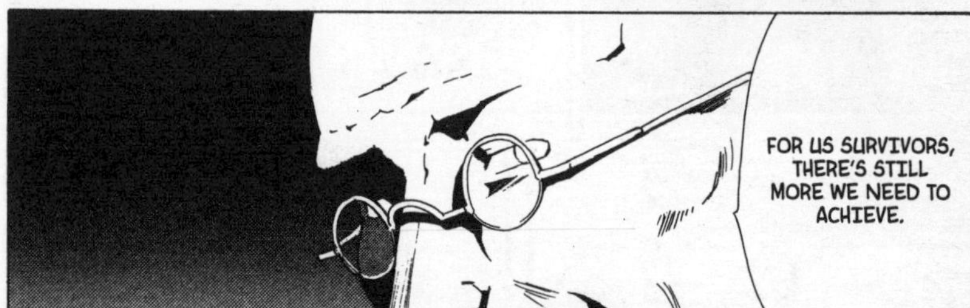

LEMEC-SAMA SAID THAT IN ORDER TO SAVE US, THE SEED MUST BE BORN INTO THE WORLD, CORRECT?
EXACTLY.

ON KUROU TAKAGI'S LEFT HAND IS A RING—THE SEAL WITH WHICH WE HAVE MARKED HIM.
HE IS THE "PROMISED CHILD."

IF WE EAT THE FLESH OF THE KING, OUR POWER SHOULD INCREASE.
THEREFORE, WITHOUT LETTING HIM DIE, WE MUST TEAR APART HIS STILL-LIVING FLESH.

DON'T YOU SHIVER WITH THE ANTICIPATION OF IMMORTALITY, SATOU-SENSEI?
TO US, EATING THE KING IS THE EQUIVALENT OF EATING A PARENT.
THERE-FORE...

THE SEED MAKES US HESITATE.
WE ARE DRAWN TO IT.

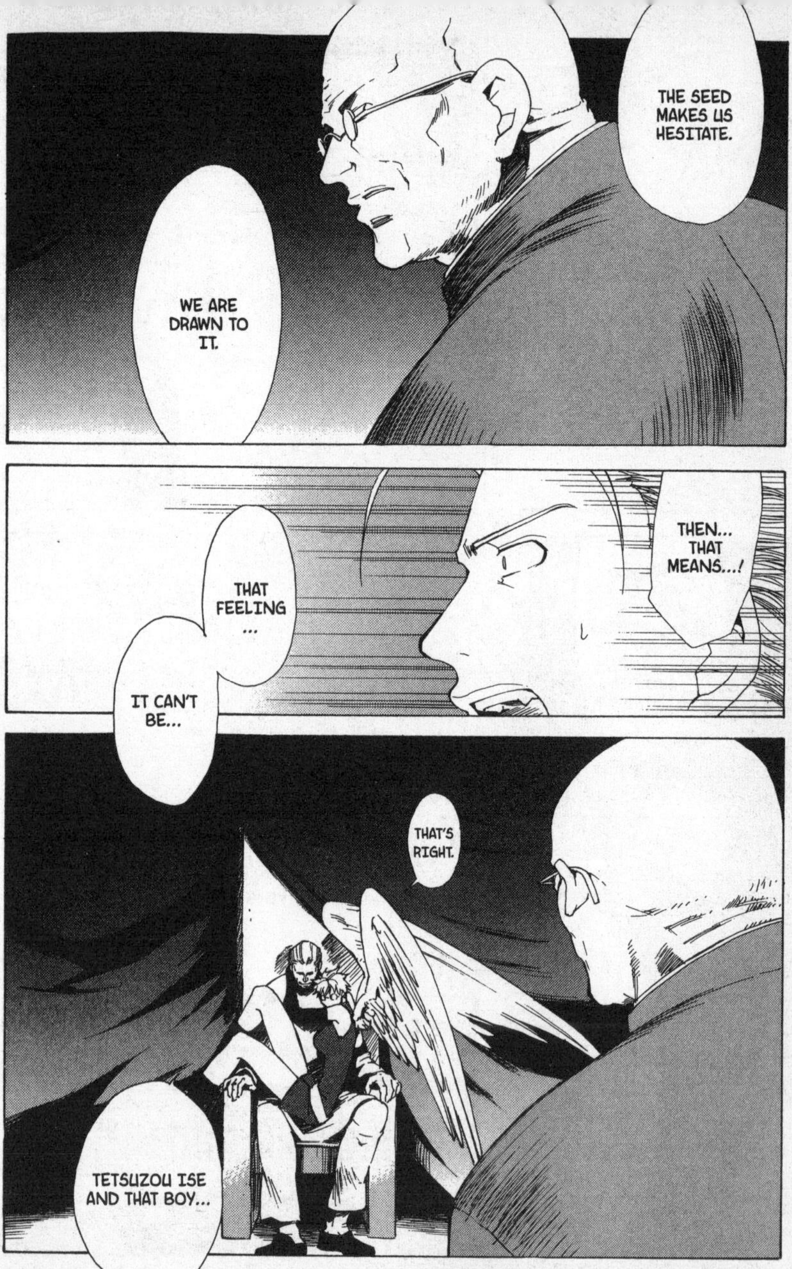

THEN... THAT MEANS...!
THAT FEELING ...
IT CAN'T BE...
THAT'S RIGHT.
TETSUZOU ISE AND THAT BOY...

THEY BOTH POSSESS NOSFERATU SEEDS WITHIN THEMSELVES.

SLIDE
SLIDE
ISE...!
DON'T WORRY.
WA...
WAIT A SECOND...!

HE... HE...
NO WAY... HE HAS THE SEED ...
KYAAA!

↕ Watches with sorrowful eyes

...
Parent's face
DO I NOT MEET YOUR EXPECTATIONS?

MUROI-SAN, WAS IT?

WHAT ARE YOU?

YOU SUDDENLY APPEAR AND TELL ME HE HAS THE SEED...

I ALREADY TOLD YOU.

I'M A CARRIER, AS WELL AS HIS FATHER.

BECAUSE YOU HOLD THE NOSFERATU SEED.

A BEARER OF THE NOSFERATU SEED IS A KEY THAT DECIDES THE FATE OF THE NOSFERATU...

THIS PERSON IS...

AN ENEMY OF THE NOSFERATU? OR A FRIEND?

BU... BUT TO SUDDENLY HEAR THAT ISE IS A SEED... IT'S NOT INTUITIVE...
UP TO NOW, I NEVER HAD THAT FEELING,
AND ONLY TOUYAMA-SAN AND I HAVE FAMILIARS...
EVERYONE SAYS WE LOOK LIKE TWINS, BUT...
DO YOU KNOW WHEN YOUR FAMILIAR WAS BORN?
...POCHI WAS BORN...
PROBABLY AT MY MOTHER'S FUNERAL...
THAT'S RIGHT.
I DON'T KNOW WHAT THEY'RE PLOTTING,
BUT THERE IS ONCE CONDITION FOR A SEED TO AWAKEN.

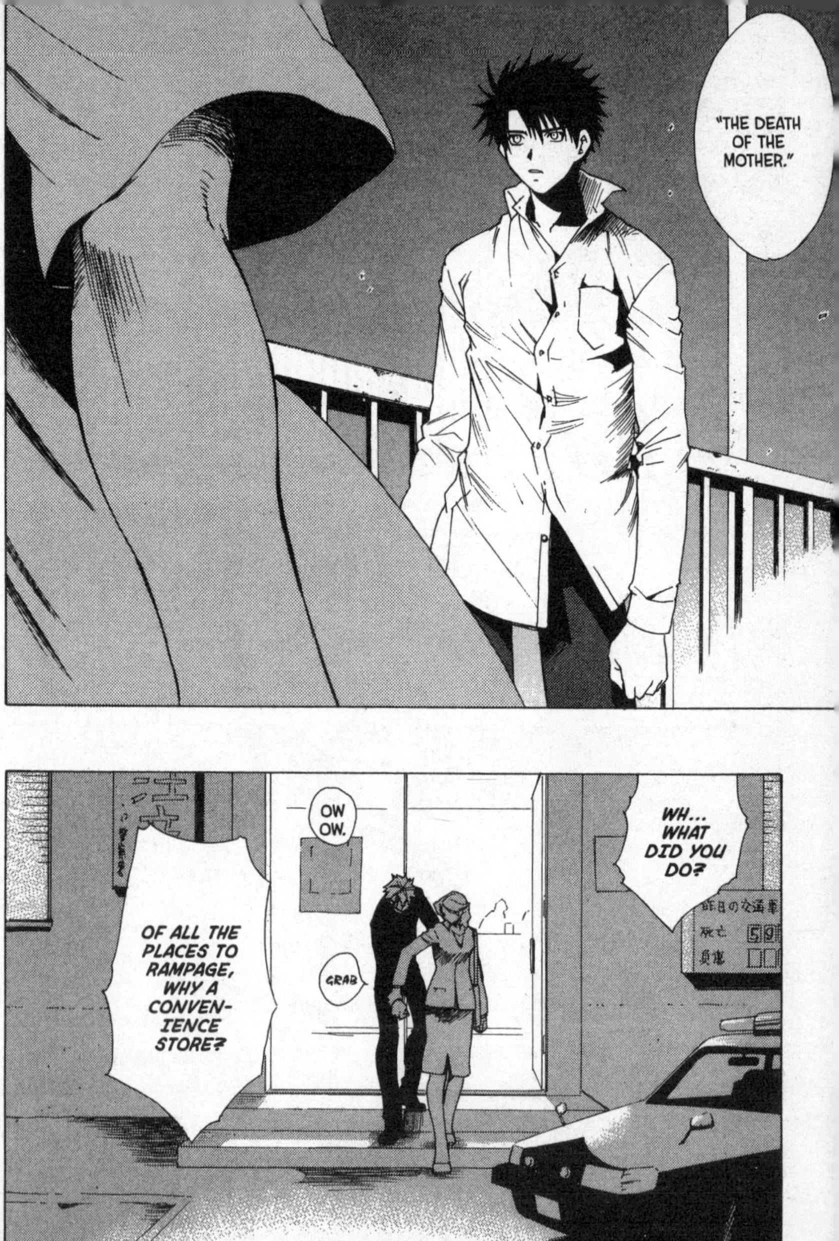

"THE DEATH OF THE MOTHER."

WH... WHAT DID YOU DO?

OW OW.

GRAB

OF ALL THE PLACES TO RAMPAGE, WHY A CONVENIENCE STORE?

THEY HAVE A LOT OF THINGS...
...

BETTER THAN STABBING PEOPLE ON THE ROADSIDE, RIGHT?
THAT'S WHAT I THINK, ANYWAY.

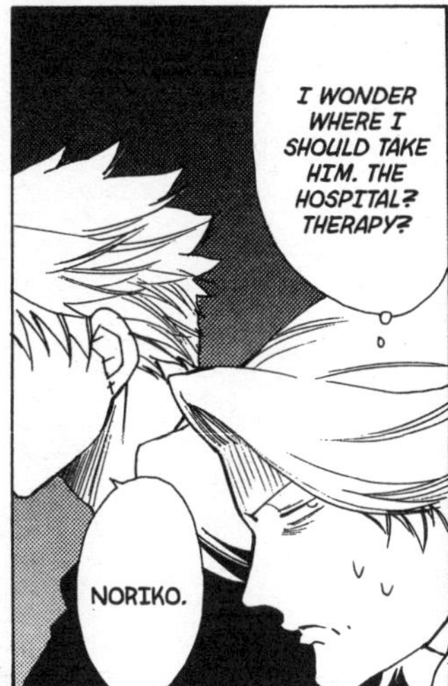
I WONDER WHERE I SHOULD TAKE HIM. THE HOSPITAL? THERAPY?
NORIKO.

WHAT DO YOU THINK OF THE SCHOOL I GO TO?
YOTSUJI ACADEMY?

IT WAS THE ONLY PLACE YOU COULD ENTER WITH YOUR GRADES, RIGHT?
AND THE ENROLLMENT FEE AND TUITION WERE ABSURDLY CHEAP.
AND THEY SENT THE PAMPHLET TO OUR HOUSE VERY QUICKLY...

I GET THE FEELING THAT MY ENTERING YOTSUJI ACADEMY WAS NOT A COINCIDENCE.
Right? ♡
WHAT?
Oh no, a romantic.
DID YOU FIND YOUR FATED PERSON?

OR YOU'VE MADE BAD FRIENDS!
Aha!
And they set you down the wrong path!
IT SEEMS LIKE SHE KNOWS ABSOLUTELY NOTHING.

WELL,
LET'S GO HOME AND EAT.
I'll scold you later.

YOU'RE STILL WEARING THAT?
THE SIZE DOESN'T FIT YOU AT ALL.

AH, THIS?
IT'S A PROTECTIVE CHARM.
And a guy-repellant.

...
COULD IT BE THAT YOU GOT THAT FROM MY FATHER?
surprise

A MAN NAMED MUROI?

...
CLOMP
CLOMP
CLOMP
STAGGER
STAGGER
BULL'S-EYE.
DAMN.

WELL, AS EXPECTED ...
HE'S OUR REAL...
HEY, NORIKO.
I...
I DON'T QUITE UNDERSTAND, BUT...

IT SEEMS LIKE HE'S THE GUY YOU CHOSE.
THIS IS BAD.
I HAVE TO HURRY AND TAKE HIM TO A MEDICAL SPECIALIST.
MIKI!
I HAVEN'T SEEN YOUR FACE IN A WHILE.
WHERE HAVE YOU BEEN?
EH? HAHAHA.
I WAS JUST GETTING SETTLED IN, BIG SISTER. I DIDN'T WANT TO TROUBLE YOU.

IT'S OK. NO BIG DEAL.
I'LL BE GOING HOME SOON.
OH YEAH. MY BOSS WANTS YOU TO WORK TOGETHER WITH ME.
Take it from me you've got a nice body and breasts.
They'll call us the Fighting Sisters!
this person...
...
THAT'S OK. I DON'T KNOW ABOUT WEARING A MASK AND A SWIMSUIT AND FIGHTING IN FRONT OF CLIENTS.
AND I USUALLY HAVE ENOUGH GOING ON AT NIGHT.
?
WHAT'S THAT? IT LOOKS IMPORTANT.
NO, NO. IT'S NOTHING...
KYA!
WHOSE UNIFORM IS THAT?
ST... STOP.
OR IS IT FOR A PLAY?!
A PLAY ...
STOP...
DROP

SHUDDER
SHUDDER
WHAT'S THAT?!
WHOOSH
NOTHING!
S... SOMETHING I MADE... Y... YEAH... A FIGURE.
DIDN'T I DO A GOOD JOB?

A BIT.
DON'T PUT EROTIC THINGS IN PEOPLE'S HOMES.
It's not erotic!
I'LL BE BACK BEFORE MORNING!
YEAH YEAH! COME BACK SAFELY!
SHUT
PHEW.

IF... IF I SPLASH IT WITH WATER, IT MIGHT RETURN TO NORMAL...

Like f... f... freeze-dried...

TRICKLE

TRICKLE

SIZZLE

RING
RING
RING
SHAKE
SHAKE
SHAKE

WHEEZE
WHEEZE
Y...
YES...?

U... KUROU-CHA ...
AH, SORRY. IT'S NOTHING ...
POCHI ...?

UH... YEAH. HE... HASN'T CHANGED FROM BEFORE.
GLANCE
HE'S FINE...

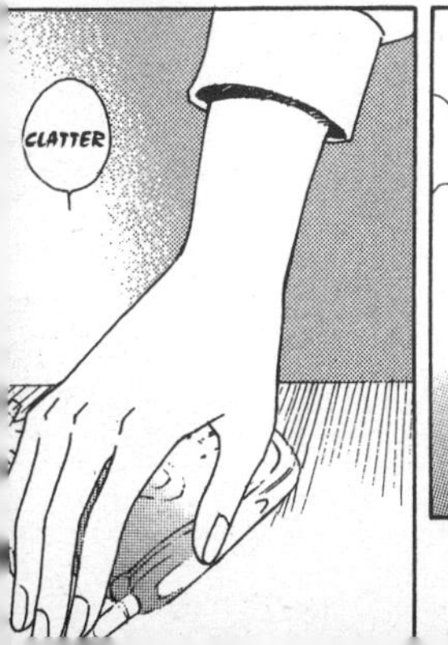
CLATTER

HE'S NOT
FINE AT ALL!

...

...

THAT'S RIGHT... TOUYAMA...

I'LL ASK TOUYAMA...
SINCE SHE RAISES NEFERTI, SHE MIGHT KNOW SOMETHING.
SIZZLE

IT'S AWFULLY QUIET TONIGHT...

LOOKS LIKE NO ONE'S HERE...

UNTIL KUROU TAKAGI TRANSFERRED HERE...

ARE YOU WORRIED FOR ME?
BUT IT'S OK...

I'M ONLY A LITTLE SCARED...

SPEAKING OF WHICH, I WAS A LITTLE SCARED OF YOU TOO WHEN WE FIRST MET.
I DIDN'T LIKE YOU MUCH...

IT'S TRUE EVEN NOW...

A NOSFERATU SEED... AND THE KEY...
SURELY, YOU'RE THE ONE I'VE BEEN WAITING FOR.

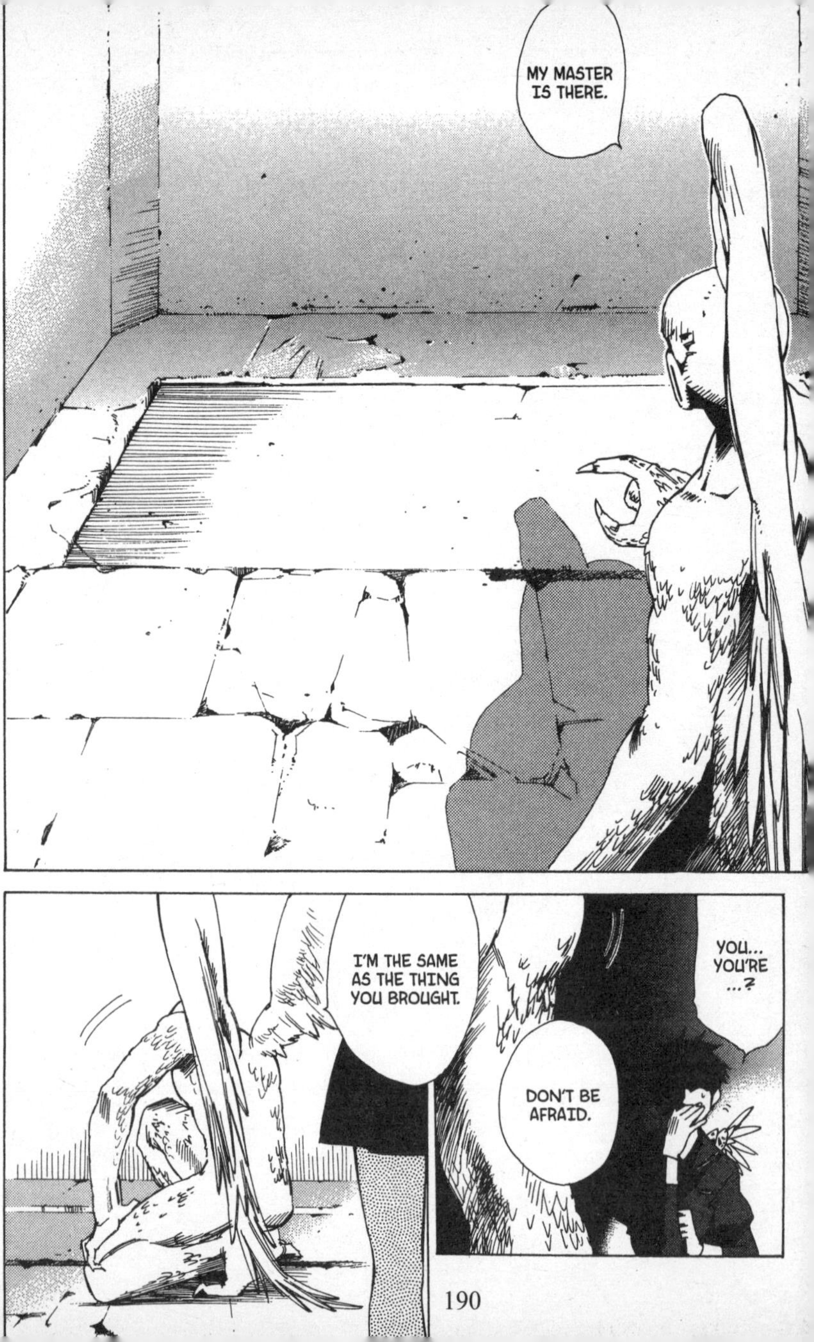

MY MASTER IS THERE.

A FAMILIAR...?

CRACK

RATTLE

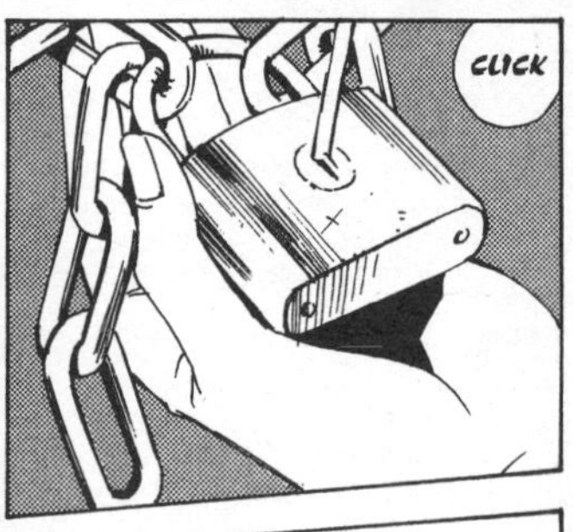
CLICK

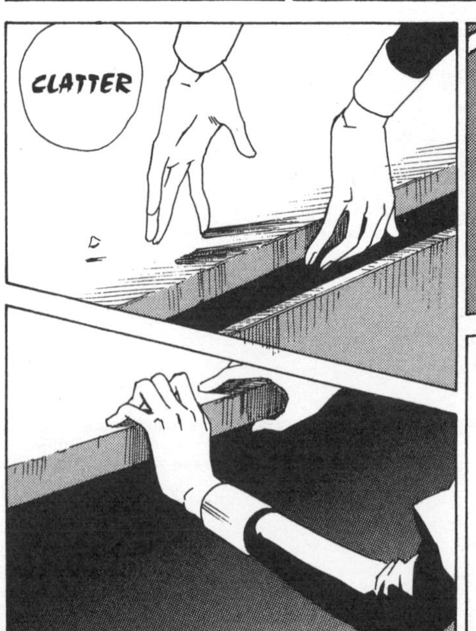
CLATTER

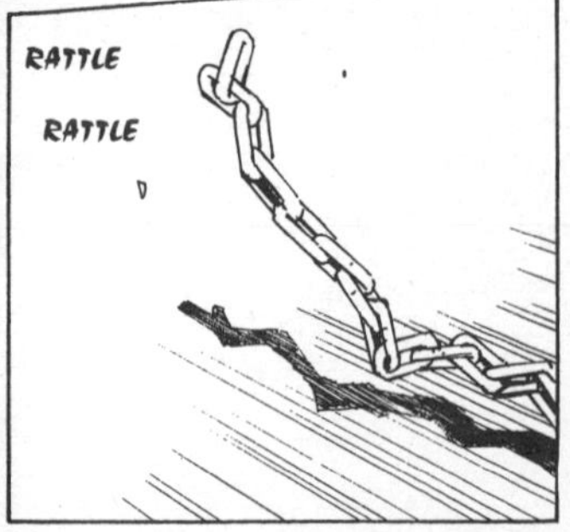
RATTLE
RATTLE

To be continued in volume nine!

© Towa Ohshima
We're in Okinawa! What awaits us as we venture into the land of exotica, Japan's southernmost prefecture filled with mysteries old and new? Romance? Forbidden love? Adventure?
High School Girls
Volumes 1-9 available NOW!
SUGGESTED AGES 15+
DrMaster Publications Inc.
www.DrMasterbooks.com

Magic Lover's Tower
by KAO-YUNG and KUAN-LIANG
vol. 1 and 2 are available now!
© by DGN Production, inc / KAO-YUNG & KUAN_LIANG
SUGGESTED
AGES 13+
DGN
PRODUCTION
DrMaster
Publications Inc.
www.DrMasterbooks.com

© 2007 SAI MADARA
BY SAI MADARA
MAMORU
THE SHADOW PROTECTOR
The story is about protecting someone you love... in secret. Mamoru Kagemori is a dull high school boy who's not handsome, athletic, or intelligent. Or so he seems. He is actually the eldest son of the 400-year-old Ninja clan specializing in protect their neighbor, the Konnyaku's. And the object of Mamoru's protection is none other than their only daughter, Yuna Konnyaku, a natural born troublemaker. Mamoru must continue to protect her to carry out his duty no matter what adversaries strong, bizarre, or stupid. And will Yuna ever learn who her protector is?
MAMORU
THE SHADOW PROTECTOR
Release date: 06/28/2008
ISBN: 978-1-59796-183-7
Pages: 192
Retail price: 9.95
Rating: 13+
Format: B/W, Paperback
Trim: 5.75 X 8.25
DrMaster Publications Inc.
www.DrMasterbooks.com
DGN PRODUCTION
SUGGESTED AGES 13+

DGN
PRODUCTION
DrMaster
Publications Inc.
www.DrMasterbooks.com

Gamers out there, your wait is finally over! All of your favorite characters are here in this explosive *King of Fighters Art Book*! Kyo, Iori, Mai, Terry, Geese and many more are present and accounted for in this collection. Original illustrations produced by artists Wing Yan and King Tung for the long running comic series in Hong Kong, have been compiled in a collection that has never been seen before!
THE KING OF FIGHTERS ™
ART BOOK
The King of Fighters Art book
Author: Wing Yan / King Tung
ISBN: 978-1-59796-127-1
Date Published: 4/27/2008
Format: Paperback / Color
Number of pages: 96
Rating: All age
Price: $21.95
DrMaster Publications Inc.
www.DrMasterbooks.com
DGN PRODUCTION
SNK PLAYMORE
© SNK PLAYMORE
© 2004 BY LION KING

SVC CHAOS
SNK VS. CAPCOM
TM
Chi Wan Shum
This incredible comic adaptation draws on characters from the world's most popular fighting game series - SNK &. CAPCOM's famous SNK VS. CAPCOM SVC CHAOS.
There exists a limbo realm where the cost of admission is death! Here a new battlefield is populated by the most powerful and fearsome martial artists the world has ever known.
volumes 1-8
available now!
© SNK PLAYMORE 2003
© CAPCOM CO., LTD. 2003
ALL RIGHTS RESERVED.
© 2003 BY HAPPY COMICS LTD.
DrMaster Publications Inc.
www.DrMasterbooks.com
DGN PRODUCTION

中華英雄
Chinese Hero
-Tales of the Blood Sword-
The only comic
with a Kung-Fu grip!
1-6 in stores now!
© Culturecom / DGN Production, Inc.
DrMaster
Publications Inc.
www.DrMasterbooks.com
DGN
PRODUCTION
SUGGESTED
AGES 13+

The Art Of Yasushi Suzuki

This project is total fan appreciation! Graphic artist and game designer - Yasushi Suzuki has meticulously compiled a stunning cache of his own work history. The Art of Yasushi Suzuki will showcase nearly 100 images, some of which were designed specifically for this event, including art from the video games Ikaruga (Sega), and Sin & Punishment (Nintendo), plus cover art from the Japanese

DrMaster
Publications Inc.
DGN
PRODUCTION
Visit us online at
drmasterbooks.com
A New World of
Comics & Manga

Wait, Don't Forget!
This book was printed in the original/Asian format. Please read panels from right to left.